Praise for
ORPHAN BACH

T0005865

"Ng's narrative might be likened to a figurative oil work, with structured lines building layers of her family's history."
—*New York Times*

"Intimate and evocative . . . Ng's grace as a storyteller makes it possible to understand in one's bones how heartless policy bends and misshapes lives for generations."   —*BookPage*

"The author's straightforward prose and the work's staggering scope bring home the myriad ways misguided policies damaged generations of immigrant families. Readers will be rapt."   —*Publishers Weekly*

"Each of Ng's exquisite books, *Bone* (1993), *Steer Toward Rock* (2008), now this, is worth the 15- year wait in-between . . . Ng presents a luminous memoir, finding transformative, aching authenticity in revealing difficult lives . . . Her exceptional storytelling elucidates and illuminates."
—*Booklist* (**starred review**)

"Luminous . . . An exemplary study of the past brought into the present, spanning years and continents."
—*Kirkus Reviews* (**starred review**)

"Fae Myenne Ng's memoir is a living history, bringing to vivid life every member of her beloved and admired family. In *Orphan Bachelors*, every humble person is the hero of their own life."

—Sau-ling Cynthia Wong, *World Journal Weekly* (*Shijie Zhoukan*)

"Ng is part of a literary revolt that argued that it is not enough to be patted on the head for writing beautifully, which she does, but like Ng, one can be the archivist and librarian of the communities' stories before they become extinct. Fae Myenne Ng continues to be among the globe's finest writers." —Ishmael Reed, author of *Mumbo Jumbo*

"Aha! So that's what became of the men who went to sea. Aha! So that's what that word—that sound—means. Oh, so I am not alone. Fae Myenne Ng's memoir helps the reader recover memories, and to know lost history."

—Maxine Hong Kingston, author of *I Love a Broad Margin to My Life*

"By turns horrifying, hilarious and moving, *Orphan Bachelors* is a book that needed to be written. I was mesmerized by its intensity and haunted by its candor; it grips the reader and does not let go." —Gish Jen, author of *The Resisters*

"*Orphan Bachelors* is so many treasures at once: an enthralling memoir, an act of reckoning, a history of American exclusion and Chinatown resilience, an attempt to conjure the vast horizons that her forebears were never allowed to imagine."

—Hua Hsu, author of *Stay True*

"No one else has written about the Exclusion era with such tenderness, intimacy, and hard-core fury. Sharp, bitter, tender, and funny, *Orphan Bachelors* teases out profound truths that vibrate with a bitter history, making my teeth chatter with anguish, curiosity, dismay. A helluva book."

—Gretel Ehrlich, author of *The Solace of Open Spaces*

"Fae Myenne Ng's memoir is devastating in its account of the human costs of the Chinese Exclusion Act and how those played out in one tough but beleaguered family. Her writing is flinty but openhearted, blessedly direct but charged with poetry that rises straight from experience. There is not one ounce of fat in this book, not a grain of self-pity or sentimentality or rhetoric. It is a wonder."

—Lucy Sante, author of *Low Life*

"Ng's memoir documents the personal legacy of her own family, as well as that of the Chinese community fractured by immigration policy. We have only to look at our current immigration record, locally and globally, to see that this story is still happening."

—Sandra Cisneros, author of *The House on Mango Street*

"Ng digs deep into ancestral bones, raw family wounds, historical and contemporary societal trauma, even exotic animal life—weaving a riveting and profound exploration into her essential self. A mind-expanding memoir that I will read again and again."

—**Helen Zia, author of** *Last Boat out of Shanghai: The Epic Story of the Chinese who Fled Mao's Revolution*

"Fae Myenne Ng chose to be a writer because, she felt, 'I had the gung fu for it.' She sure did. She's written a black belt of a book. Reading her vivid narration of her family's endless balancing act of being Chinese and American, I suddenly run into what sounds like a haiku. That's how lyrical her writing is, sometimes as musical as Cantonese poetry, other times as harsh as the Toishan dialect, employed in curses like 'Wow your mother!' or 'Dai pow,' meaning 'pulling a big gun,' or telling a good story. Fae tells a good story. Pow! Wow!"

—**Ben Fong-Torres, author of** *The Rice Room*

"Haunted by the Orphan Bachelors' never-born progeny, Fae Myenne Ng births a future by remembering them, their lived desires and endurance, honoring and inscribing their lives into the poetic songs and ancestral tablet that is this memoir. How many years ago, Ng penned the unforgettable and luminous novel, *Bone*, and today we are gifted with *Orphan Bachelors*. The circle closes."

—**Karen Tei Yamashita, author of** *I Hotel*

ORPHAN
BACHELORS

Also by Fae Myenne Ng

Bone

Steer Toward Rock

ORPHAN BACHELORS

A MEMOIR

On Being
a Confession Baby,
Chinatown Daughter,
Baa-Bai Sister,
Caretaker of Exotics,
Literary Balloon Peddler,
and Grand Historian of a
Doomed American Family

FAE MYENNE NG

Grove Press
New York

Published simultaneously in Canada
Printed in Canada

The book was set in 13.5-pt. Centaur MT Std by Alpha Design & Composition of Pittsfield NH.

First Grove Atlantic hardcover edition: May 2023
First Grove Atlantic paperback edition: May 2024

Library of Congress Cataloging-in-Publication data is available for this title.

ISBN 978-0-8021-6335-6
eISBN 978-0-8021-6222-9

Grove Press
an imprint of Grove Atlantic
154 West 14th Street
New York, NY 10011

Distributed by Publishers Group West

groveatlantic.com

24 25 26 27 28   10 9 8 7 6 5 4 3 2 1

For my sister

ORPHAN
BACHELORS

PROLOGUE

Genthe photograph collection, Library of Congress, Prints and
Photographs Division

O N THIS rare sunny day in the Outer Richmond of San Francisco, I take my late brother's tortoises down to the yard for their bath. My neighbor is in her garden and asks if I like gai choy.

"Love it," I say.

"Let me give you some."

I go to the fence and watch her cut the tall greens at their thick stems. When I reach for the bunch of bright stalks, I feel like a Miss Chinatown receiving her winning bouquet. The plumes of leaves are wider than bamboo and more delicate. I ask, "No slugs?"

"They don't like it," Fay says.

My name is Fae, too, but I don't know if we share the same Chinese character. Another day I'll ask if hers means smart or favored.

"Right. Too bitter," I say. Bitter is why I prefer gai choy over bok choy.

"Want more?" she offers.

3

Before I can decline, she's sending more over. The tall stalks double in my arms and I feel like a champ. *Who wants to be Miss Chinatown anyway?* my sister would say.

"Eat only once a week. Otherwise it's too yin," my neighbor advises.

Though my mother died in 2003, I still hear her at every meal, admonishing me for eating avocadoes, grapefruit, watermelons, any salad or raw food, all too cooling. Mom believed foods had hot and cold energies that harmonized the body, allowing it to govern health.

"Too much yin," she'd insist. "That's why you're always cold."

Growing up, this house wasn't heated. Tim, my youngest brother, put in a heating system when our mother got sick. Living here now, my Chinatown habits stick, and I can't seem to use it. This morning, when I checked the thermostat, it read 48 degrees, so I put on another sweater, proud not to waste money. When my guy, Ner, complains that all the surfaces are cold, I'm genuinely surprised. He lives off the grid in the Santa Cruz Mountains but says this house is colder than living in the woods.

Since Tim died in 2015, I've been taking care of his tortoises, his leopard geckos, and his garden. His Yoshino cherry trees have budded, and the dwarf nectarine trees are blooming. When Fay admires their tight vermillion blossoms, I turn around. Wow.

Three months into the lockdown, pandemic fatigue has made me chatty as a marooned sailor. When I ask about steaming the gai choy, my tongue feels thick. What's the word for "steam"? I can only think of the word for panfry—similar sounding—but which tone, rising or falling, lifting or flat?

Inside, I'm howling in Cantonese. My father also died in 2015. He was the last person I spoke my ancestral dialect with, and now that he's gone, there are no more laughing puns, no more witty rhymes, and no more recitation of the "Ballad of Mulan." Whatever time zone I was in, Manhattan, Rome, or outside the Mojave, my father and I spoke every night. Everyone else had had it with his pontificating so I was the relief talker.

At sea, his steady companion was silence; on land, his talk swelled like a storm. We called it boiling telephone jook, his stories like rice kernels churning in a pot. I knew them all by heart—being tricked by a story to come to America and then being swindled by more lies. Soon, every story was his vow to return to China. I listened with the phone pressed to my ear and filed papers or lay down—and more than once fell asleep.

When my father arrived in 1940, he lived at the Waverly Place, an S.R.O., one of many single-room occupancy hotels in Chinatown. That's where he met many of the old bachelors. Some had been hatchet men in their day and many still held a knife in one hand, a hammer in the other. Trust was a cautious currency. Any man could be an enemy. Any brother could betray you.

My father called them Orphan Bachelors, perhaps after the name Orphan Island, those foreign concessions in Shanghai that remained unoccupied by the Japanese, or the orphan warriors abandoned by the Qing, or closer to home, the conscripted village boys, maybe even after Fa Mulan, who volunteered to take her father's place in battle.

By the time my sister and I met them, they were defeated men without descendants, as pitiful as the deformed eunuchs of the Shang dynasty. The Orphan Bachelors sat out their days in Portsmouth Square, their silence seething as their gaze grew more and more furious. Our father taught us to call each one Grandfather.

In our childhood, my sister and I heard no fairy tales, no love stories. We only heard tales of woe. Women cried; men bled. In China, everyone went crazy from unrelenting grief or committed suicide from unrequited love. Those who survived became gambling or opium addicts—or just plain mean. In China, women jumped into wells and polluted the family water; in Chinatown, they jumped off the roof of the Ping Yuen projects, so we never felt safe in the playground. In China, butchers were revered masters of the cleaver. In America, every butcher was handsome because they were among the few males who stayed to work in the ghetto.

We learned that a story's function was to protect. Like a gung fu disciple, the easy life made a lazy student, and the hard life made a grand master. Our parents didn't believe in bedtime stories. A story that lulls you into dreaming? Why waste time telling a story that didn't terrify and teach? Stories were for waking you up not putting you to sleep. Stories were forewarnings so that we didn't venture into danger. Stories were amulets to save us from committing wrongs that could cut us down or worse, make us lose face.

When our mother told us about the Japanese soldier whose bayonet found her in the tall grasses or about the thugs at the Ping projects who dragged her friend into a waiting car, we knew not to ask why or what happened next. Curiosity only got us a dozen whacks with the chicken-feather duster. Our mother was teaching us about vigilance. If she didn't offer the story's ending, it was better not to know. Asking was disobedience: children didn't need to know the whole story.

Be careful. Be safe. Stay alive. That was the only story.

The sun is directly overhead now, and the yard is hot. In my arms, the huge emerald leaves are drooping. When I ask my neighbor for cooking instructions, my voice reminds me of slaughtering a chicken, the swift and deep slash across its throat, the blood gurgling into a bowl. My Chinese drains out of me. I think of Lima-born Alberto Fujimori, who spoke an infantile Japanese and on his first visit to Japan as Peru's president, shocked the waiters: How could this dictator order sashimi like an uncouth child?

"Only ginger," Fay answers about cooking gai choy.

I ask, "No garlic?"

She shakes her head. "They don't go together."

That night, I steam the gai choy with ginger and eat it all. I don't bother making rice, which would've horrified my mother, probably even more than Martha Stewart peeling ginger with a spoon.

I hear my mother ask, "*Why would you separate yin from yang?*"

She could have been commenting on marriage: "*Don't be the wife that eats bitterness.*"

I know her deeper worry. Her husband could have been an Orphan Bachelor, but she'd endured his errant ways and kept a family he could always return to. Though I wasn't at her deathbed, she's always been by my side. Perhaps writing was a way to hold her marital bitterness in mind and at bay, writing becoming my mourning.

When my father breathed his last, I drove over two bridges before his hearing departed, and I crawled into the house on my hands and knees, calling for him as if we were in China.

If I tell him how long it took to complete this manuscript, he might wink and mention Sima Qian, who chose castration so he could finish his long-overdue *Records of the Grand Historian.*

My parents couldn't read my novels in English and when translated, found the simplified Chinese frustrating and gave up. A seamstress who could sew up copies of dresses from sight alone, a sailor who could endure the silence and solace of the seas, their whole lives were consumed with work for the family, they did not want to read a *copy* of the original.

This teaches me that translation is not only the art of deference but also of defiance and that immigration, like any departure from land or language, is the supreme sacrifice.

Inside the home, Mom taught us to call our father Deh, an ancient pronunciation that was long and low, as if pulled from the shadow of the moon.

Mah and Deh taught me to speak and write beyond the story, even beyond translation. They didn't always get along, but they taught me how to get through life. When painting a tiger, first draw the bones. When building a house, consider the wind. When writing, consider the vessel of time that holds a story. Maybe that's also a guide on how to read this book. When reading, honor what you can't fully inhabit.

This book has no simple timeline. I've left our fissures in because what can't be known or forgiven is part of our history. I've written our hopes and disappointments, and also our illusions. I've tried to respect the unknowable and also the untranslatable. I have borrowed from life to make the story come alive on the page. "Borrowing" is the word my father used to cajole understanding. Of his own life, he often said he was "borrowing" to stay in this country, to stay in this family. As a child, I believed his stories. As a writer, I write his lies. So, perhaps this book can be, as my father was, an alien resident.

I.

ARRIVING

My father
before
sailing

My parents
on the
Broadway
Steps

My parents cooking together on Bernard Alley

I

MY SAN FRANCISCO was a village of a hundred grandfathers. This was in the early sixties; this was before the brothers. My sister, Wendy, was almost two, I was four, and our father was on land more than at sea, so he took us to Portsmouth Square every afternoon.

From Pacific Avenue, we walked down to Dupont, which was lined with old men, casually elegant in their lifetime suits worn to a sheen, their daily-wind watches on bony wrists, jade bands worn like knuckles of bamboo. Though we were taught to call each one Grandfather, my sister and I gave them our own names: Red Eyed Goong, the grandfather who once lunged at Wendy; Rolex Goong, who would come to our store and leave his watch for a brother; and Candy Grandfather, who always gave us Life Savers. I knew these names were a temporary passport before they died without any descendants.

They were our Orphan Bachelors, as common as those gray birds cooing on window ledges, and like those intelligent birds, the men saw their own reflection drinking from puddles, bathing in gutters, loitering on corners, and leaning against lampposts. I watched them carefully until Rolex Bachelor said, "You have pigeon eyes."

My father nodded. "She's smart."

What did I see? Children had long been absent from Chinatown. One by one, the Orphan Bachelors called out in a continuous song, "Little friend, hello, hello! Pretty sisters, pretty dresses!"

We waved and then continued, turning down Washington to arrive at the edge of Chinatown, to the mouth of Portsmouth Square. Sitting on the long benches and milling along the tall hedges of the park, Orphan Bachelors gathered like scolds of pigeons. Every man had the *Chinese Times* in hand. Every man shouted: Injustice! Treason! Behead Mao! Assassinate the generalissimo!

The chess tables were always three or four men deep. I couldn't see the game pieces but heard enough to know winners from losers. *Pow!* The wooden disks slammed on the cement tables. *Saat* your minister! Slaughter your king. Wow your mother!

I'm still asking, *Where's the queen?*

My sister couldn't take her eyes off the gung fu Orphan Bachelor practicing tai chi sword and I liked the one who chanted his wooden fish songs, those percussive singing-poems that made me clap my hands. Long Eared Bachelor took us to the platform commemorating where the gold rush was announced. Scholar Bachelor took us to where the first public schoolhouse in California was built in 1848 and the first American flag in San Francisco was raised in 1846. "Four years before California joined the Union," he pronounced. Where I saw points on a star, he saw petals on a bloom. Scholar Bachelor called it the flowery flag. Why? I wanted to know. Why was America called the Flowery Kingdom?

Scholar Bachelor didn't answer, so I asked other questions. Where were his wife, his children? Why did he spend nights singing love ballads in the underground music clubs, and why did he wear the same suit every day? Why and what for and how come? Scholar ignored me, so I went around the park and asked other Orphan Bachelors till they called me a mouthy bird, and one by one, they shuffled off, their steps a Chinese American song of everlasting sorrow.

The park was fun but going to Sam Wo was even better. The four-story restaurant was a narrow tower with a staircase like a conch circling into itself. Large plates of steaming rice noodles were sold in the entryway, and waiters carried food on trays above their heads, circling up the one-person stairway.

Edsel was the waiter of the fourth floor. He talked to us in English and made us laugh with his riddles. He told me he'd been a warlord in China. I wanted to ask my father if it was true, but I didn't know the Chinese word for "warlord," so I decided that Edsel was "pulling a big gun."

I loved watching him slide between the tables, slapping a wet towel to clean, depositing chopsticks, and then opening the dumbwaiter as careful as a master thief and delivering the plates to our table like hot jewels. The younger waiters came to the top floor for their breaks and their tones were almost happy, nothing like their grumpy waiter voices. They boasted and told jokes, and then suddenly, one man would crouch down and pinch another man's genitals, almost like the final twist when making dumplings. Then laughter filled the floor, as loud and maniacal as Laffing Sal at Playland.

There was always a lone Orphan Bachelor by the window that I'd watch as he waited for his bowl of rice king. When the steaming bowl of jook was placed in front of him, I watched for him to pull out a pink paper cone from his pocket and sprinkle the pork bits over the gruel.

"Don't stare," my father said. "The man is hungry."

Often, after our food arrived, I was sent over with a plate of duck. "Call him Grandfather," he instructed.

The old Bachelor's nod of receipt gave me a window of worry on who my own father might become: a bum, a man with no family.

✳ ✳

The China my mother escaped was a hungry place.

When the Japanese started bombing Canton in 1939, rice was rare in her village. My mother—the girl was nine and in charge of cooking the grain or boiling jook, its watery cousin. One day, it must have been a day of some significance, my mother—the girl had the dinner rice ready when the bomb sirens sounded. She grabbed the clay pot and ran to shelter in the mountains.

What stayed with her wasn't the hot, heavy cauldron or the gunfire ricocheting as she ran or being in the dark cave, it was that first mouthful of warm rice sliding pass her teeth, its nutty aroma filling her mouth.

That girlhood hunger followed her to America. At dinner, my mother broke down the cost of each dish: the quarter pound of lean pork, the greens, the sliver of ginger, the gas used to quick fry it. Our mother gave us the morsels; she sucked on gristle and bone, so we learned debt. Hunger had been her regular fare, so she made sure we never knew it. That was her menu: sacrifice.

I cultivated a different sort of hunger. Our father's time at sea was something to imagine, but our mother's toiling at the sweatshop was something I saw day and night. After school, my sister and I went to the sweatshop to help turn pockets, belt loops, and collars. I stood behind her chair and watched her pushing bolts and bolts of fabric through the stamping needle. Her eyesight would wane and her once-gentle voice became sewing-lady loud in order to be heard over the motoring machines. And after dinner, she'd go to her rental Singer and sew into the night, the gunfire *ta-ta-tat-tat* invading my dreaming and then my waking. I saw and felt and heard how she ate bitterness. My worry was, *How would I ever repay her?*

Protection was our inheritance. Our mother told rape stories to keep us fearful. Our father told about being beat up when he crossed Broadway to keep us careful.

"We suffered. You shouldn't," they both said.

They taught us: "Talk back. Hit back. Curse back."

Back. Back. Back. No one would tell us to go back to China.

On weekends, our father took us to the movies. The World, Sun Sing, the Great Star, or Grandview, all the films were the same. All sad China, all back there. The women hauling baskets of rocks on bending shoulder poles to build new roads, the village daughters becoming bar girls in Hong Kong. Every scene was a fight: serfs against warlords, a Nationalist brother against a Communist one, every wife living a worse life than any conscripted soldier.

In the summers, the traveling opera troupes performed at the Sun Sing and we went every night for weeks. The sweatshop played the operas and the ladies sang the songs of betrayal, treason, and forbidden love as they sewed.

Soon, I started to notice their kingfisher's ornaments losing their blue feathers and their swords tarnishing. The men who played the heroines were no longer convincing as nubile maidens; the Monkey King, who stole the Jade Emperor's immortal peaches, seemed more a rascal than a wily trickster; and the concubine Yang Guifei, who demanded lychees from Canton, was not as curvaceous or cunning as the real seductress of the Tang dynasty. She was a he, a young male actor.

My sister was disgusted by the scenes of servant girls sobbing into their tattered sleeves, birthing women begging for the rustiest pair of scissors to take into a shed. Now she won't use chopsticks, refuses to watch Chinese films, and about visiting China, she declares, "I don't need to go there."

She's glad our parents got out. "Otherwise, we'd be wearing horrible clothes."

2

OUR FATHER's elder sister arrived with her husband in 1921. We called her Big Aunt. Big Uncle was a twin, but I don't remember another uncle. My mother explained that in their village, the weaker twin was sacrificed at birth to prevent it from stealing the *hei*, the life force of the stronger twin. Big Uncle was gentle and always deferred to Big Aunt. Surely, his family married him to a strong woman to counteract any imbalance.

Big Aunt would buy the paper name needed for my father to enter the country. She found a man with American citizenship selling a slot for a paper son that was compatible to my father's age. Big Aunt paid $4,000 for the paper name so that her brother could circumvent the Chinese Exclusion Act. This was 1940. Today, that would be the equivalent of $82,000.

I've seen the photos of the three sons of the paper family. The first and second sons are dark complexioned with features that match the paper father's, my father is pale with a narrow face.

A coaching book is sent to my father—the boy in China. His paper father's immigration interview—questions asked, and answers given—is to be memorized and then destroyed. My father—the boy calls it his Book of Lies. Already defiant at sixteen, he didn't believe he should beg and lie in order to get into the Flowery Kingdom. But, obedient to his sister, he learns the genealogy of his paper family, memorizes the map of his paper village until he can blindly walk to the paper well, the paper grain barns, the paper schoolhouse, and the paper temple. He knew when the last typhoon hit, the woven pattern in the destroyed courtyard. Through rote memorization, he becomes another man's son.

I was in junior high when my father showed me his Book of Lies. It was one of those long afternoons between sea voyages when he was bored with being on land and had probably fought with our mother and was chatty because they weren't speaking.

I remember the traveling valise coming out from under their bed, how carefully he unwrapped the triple-folded bundle of rice paper, how each sheet was thinner than the tissue paper my mother used to cut patterns for her dresses.

The Book of Lies opened to several maps: the elaborate courtyard, the many rooms of the family compound, the path to the village well, the road to the market. Then came pages lined with interrogation questions asked by the immigration officials in San Francisco, along with the correct answers. He committed these lies to memory till he believed they were his own truth, but he never forgot the humiliation.

From my father's Book of Lies:

Q: If you are the person you claim to be, you have a relative who is a doctor according to certain testimony that has been given. How is it that you do not know anything about that?

A: Maybe I have a relative that is a doctor, but I do not know anything about him. I have never heard him mentioned.

Q: When you went to Hong Kong en route to this country, how did you reach Hong Kong?

A: From my village, I took the walk to Ai Gong Market, then I took a bus to Gung Yick City, then took a boat for Macao, and from there I took another boat to Hong Kong.

Q: According to your alleged brothers, there has been more or less no association between their family and their mother's family. How is it that you know so little about your mother's people?

A: I have never been to my mother's village. Or I may have gone when I was small.

Q: How is it that you came to the United States and left your mother with no other children of hers there?

A: My mother wanted me to come here.

Q: What ancestral tablets does your house contain?

A: Two. One for my great-grandfather and one for my grandfather.

This last question about ancestral tablets haunts me. Our Chinatown home had a tablet for Great-Grandfather, a long sheet of paper with his name written in the center. When I asked why we didn't have a tablet for any of the other dead, Mom told me their tablets were in our ancestral home in China because their bones were interred there. Great-Grandfather's bones were in America, so his ancestral tablet was here.

When I leaned in to get a closer look at my father's Book of Lies, I smelled sandalwood. The rows and rows of characters were like intricate knots, and alongside the complex words was the occasional red circle like a floating balloon.

"Why the red balloons?" I wanted to know.

"Trick questions," my father told me.

"If things are so bad here, what was it like in China?"

He told me, "More bleak, more broken."

I didn't ask how he bore it, but he told me.

"Hopeless."

As he brushed his palm over his face, I glanced away because I knew my father made a tonic of his feelings to store its ills inside. Regret grew into an ulcer of fury.

"Everything was written, everything was in the book." He'd already told me about the stalls of professional scribes on Dupont Street who wrote letters for the illiterate laborers. Now I learned that they also penned the Books of Lies for the hopeful sojourners. As my father refolded the book and slipped it inside his breast pocket, I imagined him carrying his lie across seven thousand nautical miles, and I understood the cost of fitting himself into the country. He'd learned lies to become the lie. Those lies made my father fit; and those lies would make my becoming a writer, my fit. I knew then that I would write those truths to make his life real.

"That's proof," I said. "You would have been deported."

His brow lifted, a dare. My father had will; he had golden nerve.

Expose. Don't explain. A writer can't buy this kind of training.

When our father memorized a fake history in order to circumvent the 1882 law that excluded the Chinese, he forgot the mother who made him flat noodles, the brothers who taught him to swim. He forgot the family's emporium of rare, fermented teas, the smell of his grandmother's bound feet, the climates his roaming ancestors adapted to before settling in the verdant, five growing seasons of the Pearl River Delta. He realigned loyalties and memorized his paper family's livestock holdings and their gravesite locations.

I still wanted more. "But how did you get here?"

"I got on the SS *Coolidge*," he said.

My father—the boy boarded with a valise of thick cardboard that held a change of clothes, herbs, medicinal teas, some seeds. Third-class travel cost ninety American dollars. The food was Chinese and tolerable. He chose the top bed of the three-tier bunk.

On board, the Orphan Bachelors called him Lucky Boy. They told him that he had it easy, that this wasn't 1820 when Peruvian ships caught young boys off the Canton harbor and stuffed them into bamboo baskets threaded with wire, weighed and auctioned them off like piglets, and shipped them to work the guano caves in Lima.

"Those were the floating hells," the Orphan Bachelors jeered. "Pig cargo. Pig slaves." They tormented him with the stories of 120 vile days. How many starved to death, how many slit their own throats, how many tried to mutiny the vessel, how many walked the plank.

"You are sailing in luxury," they sighed. "*Taan sai gaai*," they hooted.

On his sea voyage, my father—the boy recited his Book of Lies again and again to soothe his pounding heart. He listened to Orphan Bachelors grumbling about their fate, singing operas, and then gambling away their future earnings. He listened to them discuss Roosevelt's efforts to curb Japan's domination, the men bantered in dialect, and bored, stretched out the three syllables of Roosevelt to become *Lor shlue fook* (nail screw lucky).

My father counted time by counting eggs. Every Sunday, steerage passengers got one hard-boiled egg. After the third egg, the ocean liner passed under the Golden Gate Bridge and steerage passengers were allowed up on deck (otherwise, my father claimed, after all that time below deck, mutiny!). As the ship passed under the protection of the bridge's narrow shadow, every man rushed to the handrails and threw their coaching books into the sea.

My father (no longer the boy) didn't step forward; he stepped back. He refused to relinquish his Book of Lies.

Only the Chinese disembarked when the vessel docked at Angel Island. Chosen for its isolation in the bay, Angel Island opened in 1910 as a detention center to enforce the Chinese Exclusion Act. The year 1940 was Angel Island's last as a detention facility; my father was one of the youngest detainees. *Mook Ok* was his name for it. Wooden House.

When *Island*, a collection of poems written by Angel Island detainees was published in 1980, I showed it to my father and he remembered many of the poems, which were carved on the barrack walls. We went through the photographs together: a sea of hats on the deck of the ship, the triple-decked bunkers, men in loose pants playing volleyball.

I wanted to know if that was fun.

My father shrugged. "It helped to pass the day."

Another photograph: thirty bare-chested Chinese men waiting for a medical examination. The doctor, a hunching man with a scraping stare, sits at a small desk, his elbows and thick hands over a black book. At his side, a guard in knee-high boots measures a boy's forehead. Arranged by height, baby-eyed boys stand stoop-shouldered on the outer edge. The men, at least a head taller, stand toward the center of the room, staring at the examiner. My father poked a finger at a near-naked boy toward the front and says, "That's me."

Those eyes scared me. Bold, angry, and revengeful. Eyes that would make you pay. Humiliation with a vengeance.

My father waited over a month for his interrogation. He had learned his lies and gave all the correct answers but somehow, from the mouth of his paper father to the hand of the scribe, between the interrogator and through the translator, the answers got twisted and deemed incorrect.

Entry denied.

My father was furious, then belligerent, then locked up.

The window of his cell was as wide as his face—ear to ear—giving him a view of the hills. The distant pines reminded him of home, and like an ancient warrior, he vowed to the majestic pine that he would gain his freedom and return home.

Deer roamed the hills of Angel Island. An old-timer had told him that a sighting of this animal bodes well and so my father watched and waited, hoping for luck and chance. On the day a doe passed under his window, her wide and furtive eyes reaching inside the cell to train on him, he felt his luck changing.

Cooks and waiters traveled from the Wooden House to Chinatown every day and carried SOS messages from the detainees to relations in the city. No doubt this was how my father got a message to his sister, and of course she dispatched a lawyer to sort out her brother's entry papers.

On his last night in the Wooden House, he was awakened by a weight at the edge of his bed.

"Friend," my father said. "This isn't your bed."

The spirit didn't move, didn't answer, so my father reached over to tap the man's shoulder, but his palm passed through nothingness and so he knew this was a bereaved spirit, unable to travel to the netherworld.

For the first time in that long-journeying afternoon, my father smiled, and I understood he was telling me a true story. "I offered to be his envoy, to deliver his message to his kin."

Finally ashore, my father—the paper son began his American life as You Thin Toy. This paper name became his true name. I always thought the immigration officer who transliterated his name was having fun as a writer, making a sentence out of a name. One of my first acts of translation was to realize what the name meant: To Have Trust. It fit. My father never coveted gold, the element of America; he wanted hope. The name my father left in China was Ng Gim Yim. Gim is written with the radical for gold, its root means cloth and describes brocade threaded with gold. Yim is made of two fire ideograms, fire atop fire. He was a boy born into gilt and flaming gold.

In San Francisco, he had a bachelor's life, living in a room at Waverly Place, having breakfast at Uncle's Café, selling the *Chinese Times* at the Square, working those first few years in restaurants in Chinatown. Most nights, he cooked for himself in the communal kitchen, a fried egg to lay over rice that he'd steamed with twigs of ginseng. This was his frugal life until he repaid his sister the full four thousand American gold dollars, with interest.

Today, the new arrivals to this country face an unending list of laws that sunder families. The laws have dizzying forms: I-129, I-130, I-551, G-325A, forms that change names, change terms, become obsolete, create themselves anew, even as this is being written. The laws and agencies responsible for upholding them have scary names that we say casually, like BYOB or TGIF: ICE, DACA, EVL. I hear more clearly the smuggling names. Listen to them. Snakes sneak into America. Piglets are sold to Peru, Cuba, Malacca. The *Golden Venture* was a snake ship, its emigrants snake cargo, the middleman a snakehead. Coyotes led illegals through the desert, across the border. Life was and still is weighed in gold. But the sale is a sale, and the sale is a lie.

3

I was surprised when my mother closed our store an hour early and even more when she announced, "We are going on an excursion." Her tone was a declaration. Where could we be going? At nine, I was trusted to go anywhere: library, post office, Portsmouth Square, and the three movie theaters. We only left Chinatown for emergencies —to SF General Hospital when a sewing needle broke and lodged in my mother's eye, the VA hospital when my father had to have an elective appendectomy in order to go to sea, downtown for Social Security, unemployment, or immigration appointments.

My mother drew the shades, turned the sign, locked the door, and soon we were crossing Broadway onto Columbus Avenue. The colors in North Beach were a shinier red, a richer green; the smells were burnt, floral, and tangy like the aroma that wafted out of our landlady Mama Pia's doorway when I delivered the rent.

At Caffe Roma, we went inside and sat at a table by the window. My mother wanted a black coffee. I ordered that and a Coke for me but I couldn't stop wondering why my mother was paying for something she could make herself.

My Coke came with a straw, which I looked at a long time, wanting to take it home. My mother gave me a look that meant, no. She took a sip of her coffee, looked at me in a way that made me sense something new.

"You should know this," she started. "When your father was a boy, he was stolen from his family and sold far away." Her voice was flat. The story she told became a lock on my heart.

There was no preview, no prep. So I waited, but there was nothing more. I looked at the mural on the walls, the blue skies, the clouds, and the pink babies floating across the ceiling. I hoped she would not repeat the story.

We walked back to Chinatown and while shopping for dinner, I kept thinking about what I didn't understand. Why did we leave our home ground to hear this story? It took many days, but when the story settled inside me, I became obsessed with telling my father.

One night, I stayed up to help iron interfacing for the peacoats and as I stood behind her chair, I fixated on how fast the wheel of the machine was churning. I wanted to push my hand into its beating center and stop it. I waited for a lull and then leaned in. I shouted because even when she slowed down, the sound of the motor roared through the room.

"Can I tell him I know?" My voice was so loud!

My mother continued attaching the complex collar to the coat.

"About his story?" I repeated louder.

This time she answered with a mouth-sound that was a mix of disdain and amusement, as if since telling the story, she was freed.

"What good would that do?" she asked. Her feet pedaled and the sewing sounded like a traffic jam. "Your father knows."

My mother's eyes had the same distraction as when she looked at me at Caffe Roma. She had trusted me with a family story; I was no longer a child.

She stopped sewing. "Listen to me. Know his life, the cost and the crime. I took you outside of Chinatown to tell you because I didn't want the story in our home. When I told you, I saw your girl-wide eyes sharpen into a wise pigeon gaze and knew that you wouldn't become a woman fooled into sacrifice through sympathy.

"Masked thieves broke into their house. His mother fought. She begged but they beat her and snatched him, sold him to another province, into another dialect, an assurance that he could never cry his way back home.

"Big Aunt said that when he was first brought to their village, he was not yet four but already fierce. When their mother cajoled him with a bowl of rice with pork and salted vegetables, he knocked it out of her hand, breaking porcelain. His new mother demanded, 'Call me Mother. Yours was bad, yours didn't want you.'

He pointed at New Mother's bound feet and yelled, 'You're a duck-webbed hag. My Mama is good, Mama is good!'"

My mother said, "You will grow into the business of stories and you will learn: stories are dangerous. Exercise caution. Always keep something for yourself. Never let sympathy blind you.

"I've told it all. Do not ask again." Then she turned back to her machine and began sewing.

* *

I was in my late twenties and living in New York before I gathered enough courage to tell the story outside of the family, to friends who were my generation, with families from the four districts of Canton. My first friend nodded and so did the second. "The same with our father, our uncle."

So, I lived with the story but never told it to the person it belonged to.

Maybe my mother's trust honed my desire not just to tell stories but also to consider who a story was for.

* *

Our father's true birth date is unknown. The one we have is November 7, 1921, the paper birth date he used to enter

33

America. We celebrated birthdays—lunar and solar—but I don't remember any parties for Dad. I know that he was born near the end of the Warlord Era (1916–1928), that turbulent decade after the collapse of the Qing dynasty. Canton was always the hotbed of uprisings since it was far from the seat of power. Our region was subtropical with mild winters, humid summers, and monsoons. With five growing seasons, the common folk lived outside, singing while harvesting, cooking in the open air, listening to the traveling musicians and to the rebels fomenting revolt.

Every story had enough truth, every story made the listener grateful that his own was not the last misfortune.

Growing up, I thought my eavesdropping skills were inferior because I could not grasp my father's story. As an adult, I came to realize that my father never knew his full story. Like the Orphan Bachelors who were ostracized from their full life potential, my father also learned to take one fact and clothe it in lore.

Though his education was interrupted, he loved reading and collected books and always took them to sea. I have his library now, old-style books from a bygone time. The paper is tissue thin and two pages are printed on one single sheet and then folded over so that there was a hollow sleeve in the center. I don't know why. Was it for slipping notes inside? The books are bound with twine; some volumes have their own cases with closures made of carved bone that slip into hoops. I wish I could read them.

Like every Orphan Bachelor, my father always had a news-paper in his hand. I have found boxes of his clippings from the *Chinese Times* and *World Journal*. One had to only know two to three thousand characters to read the paper; eight thousand was needed to be considered educated. As my parents predicted, I've lost most of my Chinese, "returning" my memorized characters to my teachers. At most, I might have three hundred characters to my name, a literary pauper now.

As a child, I used Chinese and believed that if I asked the right questions, I would get the information I needed to fill in the gaps of my father's story. But when I asked a direct question, I felt rude and disrespectful, and he acted cornered. This was the opposite of what I was learning in English: to get what you wanted, you had to ask for it. That was how English worked, simple and direct. Chinese was indirect: should be, could be, maybe, perhaps. *Pei you* was a word my father favored. He used it loosely and idiosyncratically, its meaning was all in the orbit of "for example, suppose this, then perhaps that." It was maddeningly untranslatable and the more I prodded, the more evasive and long-winded his story became, the holes only getting deeper and deeper; I felt I was on the doomed *Titanic*.

I realized that the tall tales were the lore my father needed to believe, and I was lured into the wild imagining of every Orphan Bachelor's propensity to tell it bigger and more tragically. Whoever opened their mouth was the one holding the world's worst story. Horror engendered competition. If

35

I looked like I believed them, the Orphan Bachelor would laugh and say, "I'm only pulling a big gun, telling a good story to take back to China as the warrior and not the Orphan Bachelor."

At the Square, Scholar Bachelor didn't even call it China, he called it Big Earth, as if the bigness of land made for more slaughter and surrender.

The arguing was most raucous at the chess tables. When Big Chess Bachelor pushed his soldier across the river to attack the emperor, he cursed the Manchus who ruled for three hundred years.

Little Chess Bachelor sent his bishop down the board and declared, "Nature was the first lord of calamity. Don't forget that the Pearl River rose in the sixth month of 1885, and by the seventh month, the flooding killed over nine thousand!"

"That's true!" Big Chess added, "Those Manchus used up all the reserves to fight the Opium Wars and there was nothing to send to us after the flooding."

"Never anything for the South!" Little Chess agreed.

Scholar Bachelor added, "Not just one Opium War, but two! How much humiliation must we bear? First, in 1787, the British forced the sale of over four thousand chests of opium, which ruined the common man. Then, in 1839, the First Opium War opened the ports at Canton, Shanghai, Fuzhou, and Xiamen to foreign trade. And in '42, Hong Kong was ceded to the queen."

My father hollered, "Why did we pay reparations? England and France got trade and diplomatic status and they still refused to bow to our emperors! No respect."

How! How! How! "How those hell-face Western crooknoses cut up our Big Earth.

"Our Canton was the hardest hit." Scholar Bachelor continued, "For eighty years, we had been China's main seaport, but after the First Opium War, we had to compete with eight other ports."

Newspaper Bachelor added, "By 1850, all the insurrections made Canton hard to control, but the Qing court allowed the lawlessness and let the uprisings become uncontrollable."

The men clucked.

Newspaper Bachelor added, "Don't forget the Heaven and Earth Society and the Red Turban Rebellion in '54, how they recruited our Cantonese sons to run their prostitution, opium smuggling, and sea thievery."

"Sea thievery? What's sea thievery?" Big Chess laughed. "You pull a big gun!"

"It's true," Little Chess insisted, "King of the Sea."

"What about a year later in '55?" Hakka Bachelor shouted, "You Canton Locals attacked us!"

"Who attack?" Several Canton Bachelors shouted, "We were protecting our land. You Hakka Nomads, you Gypsy Orphans!"

"Nomad, who? We Hakkas have lived in the delta for generations! You Canton Locals forced us into the waterways and hills!"

"Your butthole! Who!" Big Chess shouted, "We Canton Locals are the original peoples. You all still speak Hakka!"

"I can speak Cantonese. I just don't want to," Hakka Bachelor shouted.

"*Wey.*" Big Chess wagged his finger. "You Hakkas helped the Japanese raid our villages. You Hakkas murdered suspected sympathizers of the Red Turbans."

"You Cantonese attacked our Hakka villages!" Big Chess repeated.

Little Chess snapped his head forward. "Who could attack your village? You live in a round fortress, all wall, not one window on the ground floor, only way in is through a mouse door."

"You Dead Man," Big Chess yelled. "You have your women fight with their big, unbound feet!"

Little Chess nodded. "So lethal!"

"Wow your mother, wow all your mothers' mothers', nine generations back!" Hakka Bachelor shouted. "One million dead from the ten-year war." He bent his knees into a fighting stance.

"Cool down your fire," Scholar Bachelor said. "We are brothers in the Flowery Kingdom, we are all Chinese."

Newspaper Bachelor said, "Who knows that our Sun Yat-sen entered the Kingdom of Hawaii as a paper son, a falsehood he corrected only after he became president of the new republic!"

"Our Hakka brother! He kicked out the Qing, too!" Hakka Bachelor clapped.

My father hollered, "Even the father of the Republic of China was a paper son in the Flowery Kingdom."

"Don't forget Hong Xiuquan," Scholar added. "He led the Taiping Rebellion."

"True!" Hakka Bachelor said. "After flunking his imperial exams the third time, he fell ill and hallucinated that he was the younger brother of Jesus Christ and that God told him to overthrow the Qing. Can you believe it? Then he burns all the Confucian and Buddhist texts, mixes up communism with the ten Christian laws, and builds an army of two million, to fight the Qing. He conquers seventeen provinces! Twenty, maybe thirty million dead."

"More!" Big Chess said. "Dead."

When Scholar reminded them that the Ming and Qing emperors forbade emigration, every Orphan Bachelor united to boast: "When you can't eat, who is afraid of a beheading?"

My father nodded. "Call us criminals and tax cheats. Which other road did we have?"

Scholar Bachelor agreed. "Even if the contract labor systems replaced bondage, the brokers were hired by foreign investors. We laborers were recruited by Chinese crimps, and the emperor controlled the legal contracts."

"Let's not talk about that," Newspaper Bachelor said.

"History is God," Scholar said. "You park-bench bachelors live in a jug with a penny-size view of the world. Have you not read history? In 1740, when a hundred thousand Chinese were slaughtered in Batavia, Indonesia, the emperor refused to help because he said the dead had emigrated for personal greed. And don't forget 1882, when America punished the Chinese with Exclusion, did the Qing help?"

Newspaper Bachelor said, "Don't look to the Big Earth, she has forsaken us."

Noticing me, Hakka Bachelor called out, "Pigeon Girl! You listen, as good as seeing. Eye and ear are our compatriots."

Big and Little Chess returned to their game, Newspaper Bachelor to his reading, my father and Scholar Bachelor continued their debate and I realized that the art of watching and listening was my training, that I was given the heart of the story all along.

Exodus was the only road for the men of the seven counties of the Pearl River Delta. Eventually three hundred thousand would go to America in the mid-nineteenth century. Criminals by default, my forebears would arrive to labor in the Gold Mountain.

4

Once upon a long time ago, America had an open-door policy that welcomed everyone but criminals, lepers, and prostitutes. The driving out began with the Naturalization Act of 1790 when America shifted and gave preference to the European immigrant: Only white persons were eligible for citizenship. Nonwhites didn't have the right to vote, testify in court, or own property.

White settlers started heading west in the 1840s, fueling America's manifest destiny, her lusty westward expansion. Over a thousand settlers took to the Oregon Trail as part of the land-seizing opportunity.

When the gold rush was announced in Portsmouth Square in May of 1848, there were fewer than fifty Chinese living in San Francisco. The news took three months to sail the seven-thousand-mile journey to China and by 1850, there were more than twenty-five thousand Chinese in San

Francisco. Men arrived like armies, walking from Mexico, riding in from New York, and sailing from Australia, South America, Europe, and China.

The Orphan Bachelors named the miners "Infectious Dreamers," men tricked into the hope of easy gold. "Coolie" was the name given to the Chinese, but my father refused it. Most likely, the term "coolie" comes from the Hindustani word "quli" (hired servant), possibly derived from the Turkic word "kuli" (slave), probably borrowed by the Portuguese in South India, to become the Tamil "kuli." My father called himself a man with bitter strength, a man with 努力, *nou-lik*, a man unafraid of work.

The Chinese could only work the mines long abandoned by the white man. In 1852, all Chinese were fined twenty dollars every month with a Foreign Miners' Tax. By 1870, this amounted to five million dollars, a quarter of California's revenue.

When the gold rush ended in 1855, the Chinese headed to the cities for work: San Francisco (First City), Sacramento (Second City), and Marysville (Third City). Naming by numbering was efficient. At Chinese Hospital, English names were quickly chosen and written on birth certificates and then as quickly forgotten. At home, busy and overworked, our parents called us by our order of birth. Firstborn Fae! Second Wendy! Antony, third! And last-boy, Timothy.

* *

After gold, came silver.

Everything in Chinatown had two names. Transcontinental Railroad was the outside-name. Our inside-name was Steel Road. This road was built with 90 percent Orphan Bachelor labor and would connect the East and West Coasts, allowing goods that would have taken three months overland to move across the country in three weeks. Before the Steel Road, ships sailed through the Panama Canal, a four-month journey, and before the canal, ships sailed down South America and around Cape Horn, a six-month journey. For a person to travel from New York to San Francisco, a train could take them only as far as Ohio, then they had to walk, or ride the rest of the way.

When I was invited to my sister's father-in-law's ninetieth birthday party, I flew down to join the celebration in San Gabriel's famed 626 area. I was given the honor of being seated next to Mr. Lowe. As the feast was served—duck after chicken after squab and then conch, mussels, a whole flounder, and then lobster—he told the story of how his great grandfather, Ancestor Lowe, left China. After a fight over a stall space at the village market, he thought he'd killed the man, so he fled. In Hong Kong, he was recruited by a crimp to work as a cook on the Steel Road.

Not a new story. How many times have I heard of fiery southerners getting into fights?

I inquired, "Did Ancestor Lowe know how to cook?"

"Of course not." Mr. Lowe laughed. "In those days, our forefathers did whatever was needed to make a living, and we Cantonese are masters at doing the impossible. When someone says, *can't*, we say, *can*."

When the mock shark fin soup was served, Mr. Lowe sighed about the imitation.

The broth wasn't complex or rich. The sliced bamboo, shitake, and slivers of chicken only approximated the texture of the shark fin filament. When I took a spoonful, the mouthfeel was off.

Mr. Lowe said, "Not smooth, not silky."

I agreed. This tasted nothing like my mother's shark fin soup.

Mr. Lowe continued, "On the Steel Road, each team of twenty Chinese Rail Men hired their own cooks. Otherwise, how would they get the energy to move a mountain? Not from potatoes!"

I refused to say the name of the robber baron for which Stanford is shamefully named, that he began construction of the Transcontinental Railroad in 1864 but couldn't keep a work crew. Charles Crocker suggested hiring the Chinese, but Stanford scoffed that if the robust and more experienced Irishmen quit the backbreaking work—how could the Chinese do the job? As a trial, Stanford hired fifty Chinese, and though he'd paid the Irish $35 a day with room and board, he only paid the Chinese $30 a day—no room, no board.

By 1867, the work camps were filled with twelve thousand Chinese digging and hauling dirt, breaking rock, moving the Sierra range.

Mr. Lowe's great grandfather, Ancestor Lowe, quickly set up a rotation of meals: dried oysters, scallops, shrimp and cod, fermented tofu and pickled vegetables. Live chickens and slaughtered pigs were delivered from San Francisco; mustard greens, bok choy, and water spinach were grown and harvested at the campsite or sent in from Second City. He boiled their drinking water and had a tea wagon of fresh tea always available; the Chinese Rail Men rarely got dysentery. He made fresh soy milk for breakfast and sweetened it for a snack.

The Chinese Rail Men were given the more dangerous work, longer hours and were paid less than the white Rail Men. After an extremely brutal winter of 1867, the Chinese organized. Monday, June 26. The Chinese Rail Men did not pick up their tools. "Imagine," Mr. Lowe said. "Some two thousand Chinese men strolling, chatting, drinking tea as if it were their Sunday. They demanded to be paid like the white man, to work their eight-hour day, not the Chinese twelve, and they wanted no more beatings, as the whites were never beaten. They wanted what was fair."

Their calm and determination stunned Crocker. He knew that if it were the white workers striking, there would have been a riot. Crocker conceded two dollars. The Chinese insisted on equal pay. Crocker refused and blocked transportation, cutting off all food delivery for a week, forcing the Chinese Rail Men back to work.

Food is God. We are people of famine, drought, and hunger. Our daily greeting to kin: "Eat yet?"

Mr. Lowe understood the bind: what was scarier—the danger of the work or the anger of not having money to send home? He said, "The Chinese Rail Men didn't get more, but they got something more valuable, Crocker was terrified."

I could hear my father, *We Chinese paau zai that Crocker!*

It took me a long time to come up with a translation that had my father's wit and fire: "We Chinese blew Crocker's mind."

When the project was near completion, Crocker pitted the mainly Chinese crew of the Central Pacific against the mainly Irish crew of the Union Pacific workers. Which team could lay the most track? After twelve straight hours of continuous labor, a feat of coordination and cooperation, the Central Pacific team laid ten miles and fifty-six feet of track, reaching Promontory Point to unify two of the tracks of the Transcontinental Railroad.

But what I want to know about is lunch. When the camp train pulled up at noon to serve the five thousand workers, was it the boiled beef and potatoes, and if it was, did the Chinese eat it? Mr. Lowe didn't know either. But we do know when the Steel Road was finished in 1869, it was not only ahead of schedule, but also under budget.

My parents loved their in-laws and would have been at Mr. Lowe's ninetieth birthday banquet, but there might have been fireworks. My father might have interrupted with commentary about the Chinese Rail Men eating bitterness. When he rages about injustices, his fury can be compressed into what we call *hei*, the breath, our core energy. No doubt my father would have pontificated about *kuli-hei*, coolie breath, and my mother would have accused him of having *long-winded hei*.

Though my mother would have acknowledged the fortitude of the Chinese Rail Men who built the Steel Road across America, she would have added that in 1939, our foremothers in Canton also rose in resistance, gathering all tools—hammer, hoe, shovel, and rake—to break the train tracks leading to their village in a heroic effort to halt the invading Japanese.

Om-hei, women as courageous as men.

There was a pause in the meal for the birthday speeches. Nelson, the first and only son, Wendy's husband, gave tribute to his father, who sacrificed a good life in Hong Kong to provide his son with the education that makes him the successful oncology dentist he is today. Then the grandsons came to pay their respects and receive their red envelopes. I poured tea for everyone, casting about for more *heis*. One grandson said *gik-hei* was something his mother said to him a lot. His mother nodded. "Don't annoy me."

Mr. Lowe laughed. "Every feeling is a *hei*. Just add *hei* to any characteristic to accentuate its potency."

Then, the waiter arrived with the glistening lobster, bright orange with heat, flecked with peppers and onions and our appetites returned.

The waiter announced, "*Wok-hei!*"

5

I<small>T's THAT</small> same old, same old story. Someone started the
story, someone who believed in America, and who, dar-
ing or duped, took sail. Each generation has sacrificed
a coolie to toil in faraway lands. We all have an Orphan
Bachelor here or a grass widow back there, men and women
separated by an ocean, years and years of fertility washed
away. Every family has a hatchet man, a gambler, an opium
eater, or a slave girl for which an ancestral tablet may not
have been erected.

Ours was Maternal Great-Grandfather. I have few facts
on his life: 1963, the year he died, and 1908, the year his
last child, my grandmother, was born in China. The only
document of his I've seen is a red bankbook. I was in grade
school when I discovered the thin book slipped between
boxes of dried mushrooms on a shelf in our grocery store.

Working backward, I surmise that Great-Grandfather was
born in the early 1870s. I know he had two sons before he
left China. He arrived too late for the gold rush and worked

the abandoned mines; he found no gold nugget, only gold dust. Today I have a teardrop-shaped pendant with his gold sprinkles encased in resin.

After the gold mines, he worked as a farm laborer, living in an unheated shack in Marysville, an early gold rush town in Yuba County. Years later, as an old man, when he wanted to go to San Francisco, he'd walk onto the highway, stand on its shoulder, and wait for the Greyhound, which sometimes stopped.

Our name for the 1906 earthquake was Day of Great Chaos. The city burned, but Chinatown was spared until the fire department ran out of water and then, hoping to create firebreaks, used dynamite, which only started more fires. Whatever wasn't destroyed by fire was destroyed by firepower. Four days and four nights, over ninety-six hours, Chinatown burned till the twelve-block radius of San Francisco's prime real estate was nothing but mounds of ash and piles of brick.

When city hall was destroyed, so were all birth records. The Orphan Bachelors called it an act of divine amnesty. Some claimed American citizenship and claimed American-born sons. Some visited China and upon return, claimed the birth of sons, eligible for entry, eligible for citizenship.

At Cal, a fifth-generation Chinese American told me about how his great grandfather saved their ancestral tablets from the fires. Wendy dated a guy whose grandmother was the only woman butcher at Hop Sing's and had told him the story about the herd of cattle being steered into the Portola cattle yards just before the quake hit, how they panicked and stampeded, one lone bull making its way to Chinatown, where horrified Orphan Bachelors saw it as another unlucky omen and used hatchets and cleavers to kill it. I'm still wondering, did they eat it?

I don't know if Great-Grandfather was in San Francisco during the earthquake. I do know that he returned to China in 1907. I don't know if he took advantage of the chaos and claimed American citizenship. I do know he spent a year on Angel Island, and I don't know if that was his first or return entry.

There's so much lost knowledge in our family. Exclusion and Confession developed the gene of secrecy that became the blood of our survival. Great-Grandfather would be an Orphan Bachelor for over sixty years until my mother arrived in 1953.

After his death, I found his bankbook and discovered a new world—the mystery of translation and the layering of truths. I remember feeling angry seeing his name and telling my mother, "That's not his name!"

In China, Great-Grandfather had a birth name, a school name, a marriage name, and a lineage name for the ancestral tablet; each naming marked hope and achievement.

In America, his name was Ah Sam. Every coolie's name.

* *

When my sister was born in 1958, we moved to the Villa Rosa, a three-story, twenty-four-apartment building on Pacific Avenue—just below Mason at the low base of Nob Hill. Complete family units—parents and children living together in the same country, state, the same apartment— were still rare. Twelve apartments were occupied by Orphan Bachelors, one with a schoolteacher, and another with a Sicilian widow and her mute son. The numbers told a truth: out of twenty-four apartments, only ten were filled with families.

There was a dry goods store next door that carried Chinese herbs and vegetables, bread, and milk. Every day the stock dwindled till Old Man Jue was sitting in a near-empty store. When my father asked, Old Man Jue sold it to my parents for three hundred dollars, stock and lease, the old Chinatown way, a nod, a handshake, a goodbye and good luck.

Great-Grandfather moved into the back storage room where we also had our meals. The health department found out— or more likely someone reported it—and Great-Grandfather was evicted. He moved to a room at the San Fran Hotel, a large white building on the corner of Sacramento, near the Stockton Street Tunnel, the exit out of Chinatown.

At ninety-two, our Old One, our dear ancestor, hanged himself in his room.

* *

The large male populations in the goldmining and railroad camps created an industry of sexual slavery, and Chinese women—many just girls—were smuggled in to work the brothels of the Sierras and the saloons of the Barbary Coast. In San Francisco's Chinatown, St. Louis Alley was the deplorable walkway where slave girls lived in cot-sized cages, working till they died of disease.

Ulysses Grant started to work on banning the entry of Chinese women to the country. In his Seventh Annual Message to the Senate and House of Representatives in 1874, he called Chinese women evil and claimed that their immorality threatened the institution of marriage in America. In 1875, the Page Act excluded Chinese women under the assumption that they were all prostitutes.

Grant's crusade against the Chinese broadened, and a lineup of legal restrictions followed with the intent to close America's open borders. Between 1844 and 1869, America participated in the "unequal treaties" system in China, stipulating that there was no reciprocity in travel and residence requirements. Lincoln's appointed ambassador to China, Anson Burlingame, believed in the rising equality of China and brokered a treaty that removed America from that unfair system and in 1868, China and America had full equal relations in all things, including travel and residence.

But the driving out and violence against the Chinese continued across the country as the movement "The Chinese Must Go" accelerated.

In 1882, the Chinese Exclusion Act was passed.

1882 destroyed the Burlingame Treaty and threw the United States back into the unequal treaties system in China.

1882 was the first law to ban a nationality from the United States, and it also declared the resident Chinese ineligible for citizenship.

1882 was America's first legislative victory for labor.

In 1892, the Chinese Exclusion Act was renewed for ten more years.

From 1899 to 1901, the Boxer Rebellion's power rose and its anticolonial, anti-Christian, antiforeign movement created an international anger that fueled the Chinese Exclusion Act's permanence.

In 1902, the Chinese Exclusion Act was made permanent.

The Chinese Exclusion Act would remain law till 1943.

The Chinese Exclusion Act severed families in both practice and idea. Sixty-one years of Exclusion effectively destroyed the birthing of Chinese Americans for generations.

Like many Orphan Bachelors, Exclusion held Great-Grandfather captive on American soil. Exclusion stripped Great-Grandfather of his free will to enjoy intimate relations with his wife, to raise his children, to live as a family man.

All his life, my father raged that Exclusion was a brilliant piece of legislation because it was bloodless. He'd intone: "America didn't have to kill any Chinese; her law assured none would be born."

6

D AD CALLED it his bachelor year, and he'd worked eight long springs for it. After he reimbursed his sister for his papers and passage, he worked even harder to save up for a year of respite. In 1948, he sailed home on the USS *Gordon*. Most returning bachelors arrived flamboyant with *san-hei*, their *God-hei* granting them a hundred followers as they invited the villagers to the teahouse and slaughtered pigs for dinner banquets. Many chased the dragon before they chased women, others gambled through their savings before the bachelor year was up and then had to return to America to toil.

Not Dad. Back home in his ancestral village, he preferred to be alone. His kin would arrive early in the day and mill around waiting for him to invite them to the teahouse. Their name for him was: Doesn't Leave House.

A matchmaker had given him a list of girls but he wasn't in a rush to find a bride. Instead, he bought a pair of songbirds to enjoy on his strolls along the river.

Our mother's name was last on the list. About her childhood, she has said, "In our home, there were no men."

She wasn't yet two when her father was killed in a street brawl.

When I asked why, our mother only said, "What does it take to get into a fight? Lose temper, lose life."

Our mother—the girl remembers the day a large trunk was delivered to their village. All kin gathered at their house as if a foreign guest had arrived. The trunk had come from Havana. When they broke the lock and pried open the lid, they found only rusted tools with curved blades. So I realized, Grandmah's paternal grandfather must have been an indentured cane worker for the sugar plantations in Cuba. If there had been an urn with his bones, they would have mentioned that first. I'm still pondering what was the value of these tools over his bones?

Our grandmother was a twenty-two-year-old widow with two girls under five. Her husband had just been killed, her paternal grandfather was dead, and her maternal grandfather was in America. Theirs was a house of unprotected women.

I know of only one conversation Grandmah had with her husband.

"Another daughter," she'd said to him after the birth of their second daughter. "Do you mind?"

His answer: "Life is life."

* *

My parents did meet. He didn't say no, and she didn't say yes, and this would become the family template, indirectness, the safer and maybe kinder way to communicate.

I have asked them separately why they chose each other, and their stories come together as mirrors.

"She had no father. I wanted to give her a road to life."

"He was the youngest son, taken and traded for gold. Without a mother, he suffered."

Instead of self-pity, they pitied each other; pity arranged their union.

We like to imagine Mom as the traditional bride in a heavy headdress, her shyness covered with a vermillion cloth, and Dad a proud groom with a giant chrysanthemum tied across his chest.

"Who's the present?" my sister would ask.

But that's how we'd seen it in the movies. In 1948, the civil war was on. I doubt Mom wore red or that they could afford a sedan chair, sedan runners? Most likely, they were led to the family altar where they bowed to the ancestral tablets, then to the elders, and finally, to each other.

Bride and groom left Kim Hing Village and arrived in Hong Kong just before the Communists shut the country off in 1949. Because my father had worked in the Department of the Navy, he petitioned for his wife to enter the country on the War Brides Act and as such she wasn't counted under the Immigration Act of 1924, which limited the Chinese to an annual quota of 105 persons.

My mother waited three years. When she boarded her Pan Am flight in 1953, Dad was out at sea, so Big Aunt set up the newlywed apartment on Himmelman Place, a ten-minute walk from her own home on Broadway.

The flight had a stopover in Honolulu, and when she landed in San Francisco, Big Aunt, Big Uncle, along with all seven children went to the airport to welcome her. Immigrant families did everything in a group, not just for safety, but also for face—to show adoration and protection of family.

"That's not her," Edward, the only son, said. "That's a Hawaiian girl."

Big Aunt's youngest daughter, Maybelle, was a teenager and tasked with keeping Mom company. When Dad was out at sea, Mom slept over in Maybelle's bedroom. From Big Aunt, Mom learned to make many of the famed Cantonese soups and healing herbal tonics: ginseng for energy, lamb brain (with the skull) for alertness, shark fin for winter warmth, bird's nest soup for our complexion, and finely ground freshwater pearl for my sister's alluring lash line. As a teenager, I rebelled against the bowls of bitter *dong quai* Mom made when we entered menarche. Now, I'm grateful, as my mother said I would be, especially for her ginseng tonics that still give me an extraordinary stamina.

When Mom started staying alone at their apartment, Maybelle was sent over for breakfast. As Mom steamed the dishes, the windows fogged, and Maybelle wrote out English words for her to learn. Soon, Mom would play Friar

Lawrence for Maybelle and her beau, then a jazz saxophonist, but who became the prosecutor of the gruesome homicides in the Santa Cruz Mountains, coining it the "murder capital of the world." But Peter was Korean American and in Big Aunt's eyes, being "not-Chinese" was a crime. If Mom heard a pebble thrown at the window, she would find Maybelle so that the young lovers could rendezvous.

Recently I asked Maybelle what memories she had of my father. She said, "None until your mother arrived. He must have been living at one of those bachelor hotels."

I was amused. A man did not exist until there was a wife.

The photos I have of Mom and Dad as a young couple are of them in the home, sitting together, looking at their goldfish or listening to the radio. Many are of them cooking meals. There is one that I love for its calm. My mother wears a white apron with a red ruffle trim that she sewed herself. A silk scarf protects her hairdo. My father peeks under the steamer's lid. I can see the short tail of the flounder curling over the plate's edge, can almost make out the shadow of the dorsal fin. My mother holds a spray of slivered scallions, ready to scatter for the final infusion. Their expressions are perfumed with hope, an unkind preamble to what would become a mercurial marriage. Was it Maybelle who witnessed this tender moment?

Hunger and dislocation were the common winds that my father and mother sailed by. They were compatible in only one belief: catastrophe. But even in their common suffering, they were competitive. Dad bellowed about the atrocity of nineteenth-century America. Mom countered that nothing compared to the brutality of Japan's imperial army.

Decades later, Dad would bring her a rice cooker from Japan—before it became a fad and widely available to the masses. We were also the first to have ramen, which Mom broke into four quarters and quick-cooked for our breakfast. All the Villa Rosa ladies would pack into our small kitchen to ogle the pearly white pot from Yokohama. Coquettish Mrs. Yee giggled at the thought of something Japanese in her presence; Mean Miss Luday scowled. I was chosen to click the red tab and we—daughters, sisters, mothers, and wives—waited while the steam billowed and gurgled, and our small kitchen heated up with anticipation. When it shut off with a *tock*, everyone pushed forward for a taste. I was entranced with how my mother held the bowl cupped in her palm, how gently her lips touched the porcelain rim, how with a slight flick of her wrist, the grains slid into her open mouth.

I could imagine the girl in the mountain cave: soil under her nails, dirt in her hair, low on her haunches, chipped bowl to her face. And as her first girl in America, I saw how she carried this treasured joy from Japanese-occupied Canton to our American Chinatown.

Obedience had been my mother's road, desire her heartbeat. But the acid in her marriage would become profound. She had not known how to keep something for herself and would learn how sacrifice can sour. Cold strangers and then burning rivals, my parents had no common ground except for loss.

My mother wouldn't forget the first time she saw a letter written by the father she barely remembered, his calligraphy like lace, like wire—a weave of strokes and dips, bars like arms reaching—to embrace and imprison.

Meals harmonized their union. When he returned from a forty-day voyage, she prepared an extravagant vegetarian feast: water spinach, bitter gourd, lotus root, lily bulbs, and crunchy wood mushrooms. When she was traumatized after discovering her grandfather's body, he went to Hong Kong and smuggled back the snake gall to revitalize her courage.

Early tastes are never forgotten. Recipes are eternal—blueprints of love.

* *

Tao Tao was our favorite banquet hall. The ideogram *tao* means happy and the doubling—*tao tao*—underscored the happy beat that would evade our family. It's also the name of the grand chancellor of the Eastern Tang dynasty, a poet and a warlord whom Dad revered. At the summer operas, he was the white-faced villain, maligned as cunning and deceitful.

On the crimson walls of the inner dining room were large photographs of early Chinatown. Arnold Genthe's prints are among the only records of Chinatown before the earthquake. He often hid his camera because the Chinese didn't want their images captured. As I sat under the posters, I felt a conflicted sense of pride and shame, our ancestors were curiosities even to us. Which Chinatown kid didn't pose under these black-and-white frames with confusing feelings of loyalty and betrayal? There's the toy peddler with his wheelbarrow of trinkets, the sword dancer, the fish dealer's daughter, and the paper collector. But the one that always stopped my breath was of Ross Alley. The short, tight lane is packed with Orphan Bachelors in black tunics and pants. The men are strolling, smoking, and snaking through the walkway. This is a timeless composition: this uniformity of laborers, this loneliness of the male-dominated Orphan Bachelor societies.

I knew that dark pour of men that flowed like river dirt down every alleyway; I knew what the men smoked, what their hands reached for underneath their padded tunics. I didn't and still don't and won't ever need that photo. I knew why their faces were stilled with fury and why their eyes had that hostile stare. I spoke their dialect: I could translate their silence.

The Orphan Bachelors' never-born progeny have always haunted me. The sons and daughters they couldn't have, I chose not to have. Exclusion deprived me of my sexual abundance. Sex was my biological gift for pleasure and for self but never for family. Exclusion killed my desire for progeny, for entry into that community of delusional immortality.

I made childlessness my birthright. Even if our family eluded Exclusion's barren punishment, we did not escape unscathed. If my father railed against the sexual damage done by these laws, my mother was furious that out of four, only one procreated, and not a daughter.

Our mother demanded, "What's to become of this family?"

After all her effort brewing the tonics to boost my reproductive wealth, she accused me of squandering her love. I was a thin girl with stick arms and legs and always cold. I had chaotic menstrual cycles. My periods were muscle-cramping, debilitating, fetal-spastic, wrenching marathons. When the tonics had no effect, Mom made me suck on a dense and sticky mud-ball of medicine that, after half a day of bitterness, barely dissolved from jawbreaker to Milk Dud. The medicine was awful but my agonizing cramps were gone.

Exclusion stained our family's hope for everlasting respect. Our ancestral tablets may not have a home after me. If it takes five generations to complete the trauma of alcoholism, how many generations can we afford to bleed out our trauma of Exclusion?

7

I WAS four when I started at Jean Parker Elementary School. American school was for learning the barbarian's language. English was for reading maps, pointing out freeway exits, and interpreting documents from the government or translating at the unemployment and Social Security offices. English was for helping my parents.

In Mrs. Rice's fourth grade, English became fun, shield and sword in my mind. I wrote fantastical tales where I was a magic gung fu girl who scaled buildings and swept down from rooftops to slaughter the bad boys. Mrs. Rice told me I should be a writer.

Miss Schmidt was my toughest teacher. Her round glasses magnified her unblinking owl eyes. She wore a metal brace on one leg that clanked as she limped between our seats because it had the same *sleet, sleet* sound that butchers made when they sharpened their cleavers. When Miss Schmidt passed by my chair, I tucked in as far under my desk as possible, wanting to crawl under the table as if it were an earthquake drill.

This was the early sixties, and there was no such thing as bilingual hand-holding. Miss Schmidt's voice hissed when once, reading aloud, I came upon the word "Europe," a place so foreign, the spelling so odd, I pronounced it "Ear-oop."

The day I hadn't memorized my number 7 multiplication table, Miss Schmidt screeched like a fire siren, calling out my name. I walked up to her desk very slowly and then stood as far away as I could while she glared at me over her dark frames.

Then she stood and towered over me and bellowed, "Are you joining the burlesque dancers on Broadway?" When she flung her arm, I felt myself flying out onto Broadway, running pass Carol Doda's blinking tits, trying to escape Miss Schmidt's disdain.

"Go back to your seat." Her scolding brought me back to the room.

I heard her sigh, and after that came the words that I still hear today: "Your poor, poor, hardworking parents."

When American school let out at two thirty, my sister and I had an hour for chores before we walked the two blocks to Chinese school. All Chinatown churches offered Chinese language and culture lessons. Old St. Mary's was the first cathedral in San Francisco, and when built in 1854, was the tallest building in California. All churches—Lutheran, Methodist, Baptist, even Mennonite—offered Chinese lessons. Mine was run by Presbyterians. Mom gladly paid the five dollars a month for this "childcare."

Dad was suspicious. "Tricky Christians. Don't indoctrinate my girls with *Yeh Wor Wah* God stories."

"They're making friends," Mom countered. "Let them have fun."

On Monday, we studied Chinese culture, Confucius. Tuesday was science, how the Chinese invented the first astronomy telescope, the first printing press. Wednesday was history, all about the barbarian territories conquered by emperors and the indentured slaves entombed while building the Great Wall. Thursday was poetry. Fridays were for the Bible. Miss Tsai, the pastor's wife, came to read the scripture and teach us prayers. All I remember was that she was always pregnant. After a week of so much school, I didn't want to sing "Jesus Loves Me."

In English school, we were obedient, polite, and respectful. In Chinese school, we were firecrackers. We talked back. We never shut up. We had cheat sheets: scribbles of English phonetics alongside the Chinese characters. Our teachers grimaced at our twisty English-laced Chinese. We were Americans and we made trouble.

We wanted to play. I once organized a "kill the boys" fight and sneaked Mom's cleaver into my schoolbag, only to get caught because she needed it to hack and mince a pork patty for dinner.

Scholar Bachelor was my favorite teacher, but I had to call him Teacher Owyang. He was even more ancient in the classroom than in Portsmouth Square. His large head housed hundreds of the golden poems of the Tang dynasty. He stood for the whole two hours, hardly shifting his weight as the ancient poems droned out of him like graveyard mud. We did our best to recite in the colonized Cantonese of British-controlled Hong Kong, but our mashed-up, American-accented Cantonese probably made him ill. When he shamed us for our rural dialect, we called him Frankenstein.

At six o'clock, the bell rang, he reached for his hat, and we stood up, bowed, and said in unison, "Good evening, Teacher Owyang."

I watched him gathering his books and buttoning his suit jacket, which became the maître d' suit for his night job at the Empress of China. Once, when we were invited there for a banquet, I saw him and bowed. I was surprised at his straight teeth. My parents smiled back when he said, "Obedient student."

The first time I thought about writing a story was after Teacher Owyang died. He'd fallen down the stairs at his S.R.O. hotel. At his wake, I paid respects as his standby granddaughter. How old was I? Too old to be afraid, even though I was. My parents took me home before going on to the cemetery. I stood in the entryway of our apartment, looking at the rack with our shoes: my father's army boots, stiff with their steel toes, his fancy Florsheim shoes, my mother's work flats next to her heels, my own school shoes and sneakers next to my sister's moccasins, the bells shiny and gold, and our house slippers on the lower rack. Shoes: old and new. Shoes: for outside and inside. Shoes for life: on your mark, get set, go! Then the thought popped into my head: why not write a story about Teacher Owyang? Thinking about it relaxed me and I wasn't afraid. Just pen to paper, just the thought of a story swimming inside me. I was too young to know what a story was; all I knew was that the idea fit perfectly in my head.

Miss Schmidt and Teacher Owyang were my two sincere, tyrannical grand masters. Beyond teaching me different languages, Miss Schmidt taught me to look back at my parents with gratitude, and Teacher Owyang taught me to look further back to the old country for inspiration.

Though my math skills are still poor, I never became a fan-tan dancer. I can still recite the Lord's Prayer in Cantonese, and on a magazine assignment in Beijing, I recited Li Po's "Night Thoughts" and the beginning of Po Chu-I's *The Song of Everlasting Sorrow*.

As I swam between the languages, I wrote stories in English and Chinese. I showed my Chinese stories to my father and sat by his elbow, watching him correct my characters, rebalance my sentences, his bold strokes partnering my wobbly ideograms. I remember how it felt not agreeing with every change; it was the beginning of having a sense of my own story. It would take a long time for me to realize that my father was teaching me how to let writing go, how to let my writing bloom.

I would never live in Chinese, and my father would never live in English, but in that moment, we were companions in one language. When I first started to write in English, I wrote an equal number of passages in Chinese, which I stubbornly refused to translate. No teacher could guide me through why this was necessary; I had to teach myself to trust instinct, to harness a bold unquiet: not everything can be translated.

I found inspiration in other places, with other writers. At Cal, I sat in Czeslaw Milosz's poetry class, and after realizing his teaching method was similar to Teacher Owyang's, I left. Did I believe one could only have one grand master? Years later, when I read Milosz's thoughts on literature, I felt a sense of simpatico: "Literature is born out of the desire to be truthful—not to hide anything—and not to present oneself as somebody else. Yet when you write there are certain obligations, what I call laws of form. You cannot tell everything."

I realized that this was exactly what the Orphan Bachelors had been teaching me. Escaping to New York was the only answer to my overwhelming need to be freed from the debilitating witness of my parents' hard lives. How childish and how selfish I was.

* *

My mother was a teacher in pre-Communist China, so it's no coincidence that I am also a teacher. Her inspiration was Mencius's widowed mother, who believed that her son learned from his surroundings. When they lived next to a graveyard, her son mimicked the gravediggers, shoveling and playing in the dirt. She moved them to town near a market, and her son mimicked the merchants, hawking and haggling. Moving again, this time near a school, her son studied. But he also learned truancy, and when she found out, she sliced through her weaving to teach Mencius the danger of not finishing a job, which is of course what my mother taught me, finish the job, no matter how disagreeable. Shocked, young Mencius changed his ways, studied hard, and would become, alongside Confucius, one of China's leading philosophers.

That was my mother's story: place.

My father felt the responsibility I bore and wanted to give me privacy—almost impossible in our crowded one-bedroom apartment. He made me my first office by drilling a hole along the frame of the bedroom doorframe, and with the insertion of a short cylinder pin, I locked out my consuming world of responsibility. No more noisy and needy siblings. The smallest table just fit between the door and my parents' bed; it was my kingdom of quiet.

Every afternoon, I hurried through my chores, washed the rice, cut the vegetables for dinner, and swept the apartment. I got baby Tim to nap on the sofa and then I'd wait for Mr. Jow, our neighbor, to get off his shift as a janitor at the Fairmont. He always brought me the newspapers left behind by hotel guests. I'd take them all—the *San Francisco Chronicle*, the *News-Call Bulletin*, the *Examiner*—into my "office," lock myself in, lock everyone out, and just read in golden bliss till Mom yelled for help getting dinner.

I scoured the papers for stories about murderers and robbers and crazy people. Reading about crime, I wondered why people did what they did. I learned about suspense, about all the answers we didn't have, and about the facts that we didn't believe. As my curiosity about the outside world grew so did my secrecy about our inside world. What questions to ask. Why didn't this happen? Why did that happen?

The story I never forgot was about a Chinese man in Chicago who had been locked in a mental institution for decades. He only spoke Chinese, and no one got him a translator. All he could say in English was, "Me no crazy." Year after year, he repeated his only English sentence, but it wasn't powerful enough to free him.

Jonathan Spence's *The Question of Hu* had a similar story. A man named Hu is employed by a priest and taken to France in 1678. Hu doesn't speak French and for unknown reasons is imprisoned for years. We meet him at the prison. Hu is in tattered clothes that barely cover his thin frame. He didn't rail against injustice or decry his ill treatment; he quietly and forcefully brought the story back to himself. He just wanted the story. "Why?" he asked. "Why am I locked up?"

I read this as the core question of every Orphan Bachelor. They sincerely don't understand why bad luck befalls them, but they find a way to live with the condition. My parents did the same. The marriage was pained but they stayed together. My father kept retelling stories of how good and smart and favored he was: the captain picked him to steer the ship, the boss chose him to keep the keys. Only him, the only Chinese given special status.

My father and I believe in telling the story right. We share this delusion: if we tell it right, we will be understood.

In my office, I had the privacy to swim in all that I didn't understand. My father nurtured this desire, as did my extended family of loners: Great-Grandfather, all my Orphan Bachelors, everyone a grand master at being alone.

When I chose writing, it was as if I'd been in training all my life; as the Orphan Bachelors would say, I had the gung fu for it. I'd sharpened my weapons, my ability to be alone was keen, I wasn't afraid of hard work and I had story in my bones. I didn't have to make anything up, but my anger and grief and witness made me able to imagine more than I knew. The desire to write only added to my profound desire to be alone.

* *

Since returning to California in 2008, I've been teaching at UC Berkeley. In each classroom, I've tried to re-create that first sanctuary my father made for me in the hopes a new generation of writers will feel nourished.

My favorite classroom is in the Hearst Annex. B5 sounds like a bomber jet and this freestanding bungalow runs out onto a large garden. The Hearst Memorial Gymnasium sets it away from the campus proper and I make sure class finishes in the garden with a mock cocktail party. The Campanile is in full view and when its 6:00 p.m. medley rings out, it seems to be directed straight at our garden party.

At the start of each semester, I take a linguistic inventory. "What's your first language? In which are you the most honest, the most playful?"

Many raised by grandparents speak their home languages, Cantonese, Hmong, Hokkien, Japanese, Khmer, Korean, Laotian, Mandarin, Mien, Taiwanese, Vietnamese, various dialects from India and the Philippines, and one from the Kingdom of Tonga. If they're not linguistically fluent, they're culturally fluid, skilled at deciphering volume, tone, and the clucking silences.

More have parents who refuse to speak anything but English. Sometimes, when my students open their mouths, I cringe. "If I put my head down, everybody sounds white. Why the AP speak? Why don't I hear your ancestral language in your English?"

No one can tell me.

During the pandemic lockdown, when there's a rise in Asian hate crimes, I change the course of my class. After the Atlanta shooting, we consider the fact that six out of eight killed were women of Asian descent, that that term, as used by the media, infers deviant sex. When Xiaojie Tan, the owner of Youngs Asian Massage, is named, there's no mention of tui na, which uses acupuncture energy meridians to let the life force—the *chi*—flow. No one talks about sex as a life force. The media's term "women of Asian descent" is a woeful, clumsy attempt at inclusion, but to my ears, only underlines exclusion.

They don't know that blaming Chinese Americans for the economic failing and health crises in the United States isn't new. That in 1893, when the bubonic plague raged in Yunnan, seven million Han Chinese migrated to work in that region's copper mines, and as they traveled, the plague spread. In Canton, seventy thousand died the first weeks of March 1894. A case entered Honolulu through the trade route and arrived in San Francisco in March of 1900. Chinatown was quarantined, food and supplies weren't allowed in, and cooks, houseboys, and laborers weren't allowed out. The Chinese were blamed for the plague.

My students are quiet. I ask, "What are you afraid of?"

I hear about the seven skinheads in Tracy who beat a friend and left him for dead and the father that yelled at his son, the victim: "What about the years of karate I paid for?" I hear about the walk-by cursing, the random punch, the broken car windows. My immigrant personality comes roaring in: *"Don't take it. Say something. Hit back."*

We talk. We stand together as a community to feel it.

So, when they tell me about the "Slap an Asian challenge" on Twitter, I ask, "Where are you safe?"

A young woman who has rarely spoken says, "We keep our heads down."

When I ask who knows about Vincent Chin, two hands go up, two students from my previous class. I let them off early to watch *Who Killed Vincent Chin?* I tell those watching for the second time to pay attention to language, to how the truth swims between silence and speech. What is fact, what is not?

The next class, they have the facts. That in 1982, Japan was a rising power in the auto industry. That America's Big Three—Ford, GM, and Chrysler—were laying off workers. That Vincent Chin, a Chinese American draftsman, was having his bachelor party at a strip club in Highland Park. That a Chrysler supervisor (Ebens) and his stepson (Nitz) were also at the club. That Ebens called Vincent Chin a Jap and accused him of stealing American jobs. That there was a brawl, that Chin threw a punch. That Ebens paid a Black man twenty dollars to locate Chin and twenty minutes later, nine miles away, Vincent Chin was tracked down at McDonald's. That the son held Vincent Chin down while the father used a baseball bat and swung until a witness heard the skull cracking. That Vincent Chin's brain bled onto the street. That he died four days before his wedding. That the killers served no jail time, paid no reparations, and expressed no remorse.

One student refuses to say the killers' names. Another, prelaw and raised in Chicago, expresses shame for not knowing the case.

"Not your fault." I ask him to consider why he didn't know.

Language, the medium of knowing, becomes the center of our conversation. I understand Mrs. Lily Chin's dialect; it's the language for lament. I've heard my father and mother use it to bemoan their regret at coming to America. I tell my students what I heard: the pulse behind the mother's sigh, the despair behind her silence. I ask them to consider the memory of their own ancestral language as an unadulterated power of voice.

Mrs. Chin's wailing is a shovel pitched into the earth, a rake in my four chambers. When she sighs, her neck sinks into her spine, her back bends as she wraps her arms over her own chest.

She pleads in English. "Wake up for Mama, wake up for Mama."

"Who's the English for?" I ask.

My student Rosie mentions her grandmother's funeral, the wailing, the eye-stinging incense that saturates the room, the howling and screaming, the dragging alongside the coffin. Quiet at a funeral lacks love and honor. The unfilial hire professional wailers. The louder the crying, the more respect; the dead need to hear their name called as they depart the road.

"Mrs. Chin seemed sedated," Rosie notes.

"It's a linguistic indecency," I say a bit too loudly. "Mrs. Chin is forced to testify in the barbarian's language."

Vincent Jen Chin is dead. I tell my students that if we are to give him justice, we need to know how he came to life. He wasn't her blood born. Unable to have children, Lily Chin and her husband chose Vincent from his four-year-old photo. "What a smart, alert boy," Mrs. Chin said. The Chins traveled to Hong Kong and adopted him there, though he was born in Canton.

Adoption meant Vincent Chin was an orphan, most likely abandoned, bartered, or sold to a barren woman. This is China's horrific five-thousand-year history of using women to breed. Even today, there's the hidden fact that mentally challenged women are used like cattle to produce sons.

"Adoption." That's the word used but it's not the word I hear inside the culture. Within my family—immediate and extended—this is how adoption is told:

"She got him. She bought him. Her sister (or aunt, or cousin, or relative) gave up her own baby."

In English, the word "adoption" does not translate Mrs. Chin's devastation. We don't witness her desperate fear of being barren, nor of being prohibited from having a family, and so when she switches to English for the American courts, her grief is muted. I ask the class: "Is her pain less profound because she's had to translate her despair from Chinese to English?"

On the Donahue show, Mrs. Chin uses English as she describes Vincent on his deathbed: "I hold my son."

"Held." Twice, Phil Donahue corrects Mrs. Chin. "You held your son."

Several students find this scene disturbing until I give them this grammatical truth: Chinese has no tense. Time is qualified by an event.

Yesterday, his skull was broken with a baseball bat. Today, he's in a coma. Tomorrow, he would have been married.

Mrs. Chin is a rebel. Despite practically being ordered to speak English in court, she's resilient in her sorrow by speaking her own powerful Cantonese, in diction, in tense, in truth. After the trial, she becomes an activist, traveling the country and speaking to crowds of thousands. Mrs. Chin, an immigrant who learned English as a laundress and a restaurant worker, will employ that learning to speak for justice. She doesn't want any mother to suffer as she has.

Vincent Chin's death changed manslaughter sentencing in Michigan, giving victims and their families the voice and right to make an impact statement to the judge.

I ask, "Should Mrs. Chin have given her statement in Cantonese, or should she continue to grieve in the barbarian's tongue?"

Prelaw Solomon moans, "Another one of Professor Fae's questions with no right answer."

Gretel, friend and fellow writer, asks what my father would say about the Atlanta shootings, and I tell her what I'd heard all my life: America is a bully on the world stage and a tyrant on home ground.

Dad again: *"Coming to America was coming to eat bitterness."*

That thirty-one Chinese miners were murdered in Tacoma in 1887. That twenty-eight were massacred in Jackson Springs in 1885. That rioters burned Denver's Chinatown and crushed a man's head in 1880. That the largest lynching in American history was when a mob of five hundred killed and hung seventeen Chinese men in Los Angeles in 1871. That the killers of Vincent Chin were fined only $3,000 in 1982. That the shooting at Cleveland Elementary in Stockton, California, killed four Cambodian children, a six-year-old Vietnamese child, and wounded thirty in 1989, which predated Columbine and Sandy Hook by ten years and twenty-three years respectively.

"Who knew about these atrocities?" my father ranted. He knew about each one and the Orphan Bachelors told him many, many more.

My father believed America's name predicted its doom. *Mei* (beautiful) *Gwok* (country). He broke down the character *mei* to its parts: "sheep" and "big."

"When a sheep gets big, it gets slaughtered." Time and again, my father would return to the Chinese Exclusion Act, the first law against a nationality: "From 1882 to 1943, sixty-one years. Four generations of the unborn."

"Bloodless," he said. It was a brilliant piece of legislation.

8

MY BROTHER Tim and I are Confession Babies. The year I was born—1956—President Eisenhower enacted the Chinese Confession Program. The year Tim was born—1966—President Johnson dismantled it. The Chinese Confession Program asked that every man who entered the country illegally, paper sons like my father, confess this breach of immigration policy and, in return, the program offered a chance at naturalization. *A chance.* When my father confessed, he surrendered and became a resident alien. The program's subversive intent was to divert Senator Joseph McCarthy's Communist hunt to the Chinese. Bulletins declaring the mandate were posted on lampposts, community rooms, and family association lobbies. Agents surveilled the streets, wandered through Portsmouth Square, interrupted meals at the Jackson Café, and checked for papers at the Li Po Tavern.

That December, I turned nine and started hearing my father say, "*taan bak.*"

Taan bak men were rebels who surrendered truth, laid it bare, laid it true. On Dupont, in teahouses and at the Square, *taan bak* was the two-word murmur, spoken man to man, to ask about allegiance. The Confession Program wasn't an amnesty program, but it sold itself as one. When a man confessed, he not only implicated himself and his paper family, but he put his blood family in danger as well. A confessor had to name all members of his paper and blood families. One confession implicated countless lives along several clan lines.

Every time I heard *taan bak*, I saw scenes from Chinese movies where a handsome criminal kneeled, his hair long and loose, his expression defiant, his back straight despite the wooden cangue around his neck. This was my father and his compatriots.

When my father said *daay bort*, pronouncing the word "deport" by breaking it into syllables that creaked like a door opening and shutting, I felt its decree. My father cradled danger, he sailed close to the wind—declaring the injustice—and if it weren't for his wife, he might have lived the life of a fugitive.

Dad had learned his English from onshore fights with fellow seamen, and his cursing made a felon sound like Mary Poppins. Our Toishan was a thug's dialect, the Tong

Man's hatchetspeak. Every curse was a plunging dagger: *Kill. Kill. You.*

"Deport" is the first English word I heard my father speak, so it's my first English word.

* *

Even though we had the Kim Hing Grocery, Dad still shipped out, leaving Mom to manage the store. FBI agents came in often and frightened her by demanding to know her husband's citizenship status. When my father was onshore, agents shadowed him as he played chess at Portsmouth Square or had coffee at Uncle's Café, demanding proof of confession.

"If I confess, you deport. If I don't, you deport." My father rebuked, "*I no fool.*"

When the agents interrogated his friends at the Li Po Tavern or at the park, they used Dad's paper name. Each man in the brotherhood could truthfully state, "*I know no one by that name.*"

I knew to keep my father's blood and paper names separate and secret. As the family translator, I spoke to strangers, and it wasn't the FBI. It was simple to keep the truth from them. It was acquaintances, neighbors, anyone who came into the store for milk or bread or beer. An uncle or auntie or distant relation by marriage could inform on our status or simply suggest suspicion. There were no assurances. Because Dad wasn't in touch with his paper brothers, we could not know if he was already named.

In 1966, after Tim was born, in the program's final year, my father confessed. He became one of 13,895 confessions, which exposed 22,083 paper sons and led to the revoking of 11,294 paper citizenships. The numbers spread like an infection and generations of the unborn are committed to paying. But what these numbers don't tell is how Exclusion and Confession worked in concert to cultivate suspicion within the community and ruin loyalty within families. Just when we began living as free legal families, feuding and dissent became the norm, brothers against uncles, sons against fathers, the hopeless battle of trying to match up paper and blood family lines. Loyalty was the challenge. Betrayal was the tricky guest in every family. Banquets always ended in a battle: flying fists, cursing damnations, never a handshake, only a belly of fire.

We four inherited our parents' guarded ways of holding fear in our gut that became resentment till we blew up.

"Your family is always banging the door," a cousin once noted.

Slamming a door is very efficient, a safe expression of discontent.

My father was a post-Exclusion husband so he entered the Confession Program for his marriage. Orphan Bachelors with faraway wives in China only had to send off letters with remittances. Post-Exclusion husbands with wives in America had to fend off chattering wives in all rooms of their lives, asking, demanding, and cajoling. Every man knew, it hadn't been easy to get a wife, so it was important to keep them happy.

Mom wanted a clear paper path to insure her mother's entry to America. Dad's two paper brothers had been no-shows when he was interned on Angel Island. Since then, there had not been any contact with the paper brothers, so there was no way to know or trust whether they would enter the Confession Program. Mom didn't want to leave fate to a stranger.

As a child, I was terrified not that my father would be deported but that he would choose to exit the country himself.

When I was tasked with filling out his alien registration card, checking yes or no had consequences that felt as grave as life or death. Every year, I filled out the form, forging his signature, because he became furious if asked to sign anything for the government.

In 1998, through the Freedom of Information Act, I secured my father's immigration records: his docking papers and his Confession and Naturalization files. The first I have yet to read all the way through, the second I've paged through enough to see blackened pages of expunged third-party material, and as I was his witness at the Naturalization interview, I don't need notes.

The Confession Program not only ruined my parents' marriage, but it also created a profound divide between us siblings. After Dad confessed, my sister and I, adoring teenagers, took back his original name, Ng. For reasons I still don't understand, the brothers kept Dad's paper name, Toy.

One name blood, the other name bought, one true, the other a lie. Our dissident names magnified our severed familial allegiance.

* *

In America, loving a daughter is an act of pride. In feudal China, there was no loving a daughter. Her mouth was stuffed with ashes to silence her birth cry, then she was dunked into a bucket of water—double assurance that she would not live.

Before the brothers arrived, Dad took the sisters to Dupont Street and told us how the street had all he needed as a new arrival: the butcher, the cobbler, an herbalist, a fortune-teller, a letter-writing scribe, "and a balloon peddler!"

Wendy clasped her mouth in surprise.

We always ended up at Big Uncle's chicken store and while our father chatted with the workers, the blind accountant taught us how to use the abacus and also let us play with the brush and ink. After we washed our hands, the men would set out milk crates so that we could reach over the high sinks; our small fingers were perfect for plucking the tiny wing feathers and peeling off the tight skin that encased the feet. They let us pump air into the ducks to separate skin from fat so that the ducks would roast up crisp. As the carcasses blew up bloaty and pink, my sister and I squealed; they were our duck balloons.

We missed Dad when he went to sea, but his homecomings were momentous. Though he brought us the world: life-sized koala bears from Sydney, fringed suede bags from Madrid, pounds of Australian butter, I anticipated his return more for his stories than any souvenir. At recess, I told his stories to Mrs. Rice, who suggested I write about the man who wasn't really a laborer but a traveler sailing the world. I began believing that his stories were like the Book of Lies that he'd memorized to become an American.

Dad often cashed his pay at the commissary and came home with no money for Mom. Disgruntled with the wages, he'd spend it on burial jade, vases, a pair of songbirds. I knew why he was upset because it was my job to write out the deposit slips: $161 a month.

Mom wasn't happy, she was already taking in extra sewing at night to send to Grandmah in Hong Kong. I was happy because Dad's sea stories made me the best storyteller at Jean Parker school: how he hailed a cab in Berlin, drew a street, then a shop, then Chinese characters on the shop sign, and then a man in a straw hat, his drawing delivering him to Chinatown on Kant Strasse. Smoking opium in Malacca, he'd missed the ship's launch and hired a helicopter to lower him onto the embarked vessel.

When our father sailed on a military ship from Vietnam, only I believed his account of the deck crammed with

American coffins, a detail that I'd later recognize in Robert Stone's novel *Dog Soldiers*. Meeting the author, I mentioned that my father had lived that scene. When he told me it was made up, I was thrilled at the marriage of the imagined and the lived.

Like all immigrants, my father's worry has always been for the descendants. "Generation after generation, it will be the children, and their children, who will absorb the suffering."

As an adult in New York, living the life as a writer I'd dreamed about, I often thought of Dad taking me down to Dupont Street, pointing out how that Chinatown boulevard held everything he needed, and how in a period where there were so few children, there was a balloon peddler wandering the cobblestoned lanes with his bouquet of old-style plastic balloons, each one etched with an animal floating from a long wooden stick. It was that Dad grinned telling it to me, that was what made me happy.

I never wanted to be the rare girl child waiting for a balloon. I wanted to *be* the balloon peddler.

9

H E KEPT his name on the standby list at the Sailors'
Union of the Pacific; he kept his getaway bag
under the chair by the front door. After walking
me to school, my father walked down to the union. If his
name was called, he had just enough time to come home,
get his bag, and go.

Sometimes he left behind his itinerary with the return
date circled. If not, we waited through dinner and the next
day, I went looking for him at Portsmouth Square, then the
underground music clubs on Waverly Place, and last, the
cafés: Sun Wah Kue, Uncle's, and the Universal. Then, I had
no choice but to walk down Kearney onto Montgomery and
toward the waterfront.

The Sailors' Union was cavernous, like the back room of
the butcher shop before half slabs of beef and pork were
delivered. Large windows captured the shimmering light
from the bay. It got quiet as the beefy men pinked their

pity-eyes on me. I counted my footsteps across the floor to the counter where I said my father's name, the three flat syllables like his fist on the table. Waiting as the dispatcher checked the manifests, I felt the eyes of the men become noses perching on my shoulder, their breath louder than my own heartbeat. When the dispatcher came back with my father's itinerary, I saw the ports where I could write him.

"Sorry, sweetie dear." I never understood the sorry. I didn't have it any worse than any other Chinatown kid; this was our rite of passage. Alvin, a neighbor, looked for his father at the Li Po Tavern or the Buddha Bar. My friend Jennie looked for hers at the mahjong and poker parlors, and I looked for mine at the Sailors' Union.

Even at the age of eight, I knew there could be no place I would not enter and no question I would not ask. I was already driven, a workaholic in training; I had to be. My immigrant parents had no patience for fear or shyness. I could have been a private investigator, but instead I became a writer and a teacher. I write about family; I teach my students how to escape theirs, that it's no crime.

Walking home with his itinerary, I began composing a letter to my father. That night, I worked on it like homework. I began it in Chinese, with the archaic Confucian salutation that I'd learned in Chinese school.

Dear Great and Honorable Father, below whose knee I prostrate:

After this opening, I wrote: How are you? Is the weather good? Then I translated my sentences into English. And I continued, one line in Chinese, one line in English, the sandwiching of languages a way to underline my fear that he might not return.

This wasn't translation; this was terrified repetition to stave off fear. I wanted to take care of my mother, and her directives were concrete: write something to make your father come home. She believed the right word could turn luck around. Being poor, we cashed in on luck; we were rich in hope.

When I finished my letter, my mother corrected my Chinese and I recopied it.

With great shame, I remember another letter in which I bitterly called Mom the world's most terrible mother, complaining that she never had time for us, that she was always working, always, always working, and that she cared more about making money than making us happy. I wrote in Chinese and then in English. As my sentences bloated up into a fat English paragraph, I felt my rage freed and the smallest beginning of the American in me. I could write anything. To Mom's credit, she didn't edit out my awful Chinese sentences; she let me send my vengeful, spiteful letter.

The wide-lined page with its alternating lines of ideogram and alphabet looked like a geometry problem. I folded it up and addressed the envelope to Kuala Lumpur, the farthest port. In the morning, I took it to the post office, bought and licked the stamps, sealing my hope that my father—and not the letter—would return.

What did I want my bilingual letter to do? Especially to a man who was growing more militant, angrier at America, who whacked us with the chicken-feather duster if we spoke English at the dinner table, who couldn't read English? Well, writing in Chinese was respect; writing in English was an audience.

"The steward came searching for me." My father beamed. "No one in the laundry room got mail so the steward wanted to see who was getting such a big envelope, and I showed it to him."

How boring was it at sea? I wondered.

Once I knew I had another reader, my English became more elaborate. Being read was my start to becoming a writer.

At sea, my father kept notebooks (in Chinese: daily records). When he gave me my first notebook, he instructed that I listen carefully during the day and at night to write down all that I didn't want to forget. The book was bound at the left margin with thick twine and opened from the right with blank pages that were rough and scratchy with a residue of pulp. Keeping his habit has become my practice: forgetting was death.

On land, he put his name on everything: carved into wood, written on paper, etched in metal, sketched onto porcelain, engraved into lychee pits, ivory, and jade. Whenever he saw wet cement, he'd find some twig to write out his Chinese and English names.

In his bachelor days, Dupont Street was lined with stalls of professional scribes who wrote for the illiterate: letters home to wives and mothers, coaching books for paper sons. My father said it was a good job. "Same letter to everybody. Just change the name."

Though he admired the letter writers, he didn't need to use them. He wrote his own letters and his hand—artistic and architectural—inspired my own penmanship.

My father taught me to pick up every piece of paper that had writing and to deposit it into several metal receptacles around Chinatown. "Writing is not garbage," he said. He took me to the paper temple to see the kiln that only burned paper with writing. I met the Paper Collector who walked around Chinatown with a burlap bag, collecting the writing paper from the receptacles. He looked like a garbage man. Only the Paper Collector knew the secret spot in the bay where the sacred writing ashes were dispersed.

This was like our burning paper money for Great-Grandfather's journey. Fire empowered his travels. The secrecy of the depository for the writing ashes was true to our Chinatown ways. And when I later learned that this was a practice in the Song dynasty, I was more surprised that the ritual would be carried and kept alive in the barbarian land by an Orphan Bachelor.

Tsang Tsou-choi, the self-named King of Kowloon, claims that the British stole his family's land and has repeatedly asked England to pay him taxes. He worked as a garbage collector and in the mid-1950s started to do his graffiti art; he only wrote his own name, his lineage names, and the names of kings. In 2003, his work was included in the Venice Biennale and before his death in 2007, he had gained notoriety as a rebel graffiti calligrapher whose work preceded Banksy, Haring, and Basquiat. Tsang's thick, misshapen calligraphy was like that of a mad monk. He left school at nine, he used cheap bottled ink and then markers and only wrote on public property, government buildings, traffic signs, train stations, garbage cans, and train platforms, he often decried the Queen of England. Disowned by his wife and eight children, the King of Kowloon was an original Orphan Bachelor.

In 1974, Norman Mailer wrote an essay about graffiti art in New York. He noted that the artists only wrote their names, they were their own subject and model. My father has done the same all his life. Everywhere I look as I try to clear the house, I see my father's two names, carved on loquat seeds, etched in rocks gathered from his travels, carved into the wooden fence and the poured cement in the yard.

In his life, paper was gold.

Exclusion, Confession, and Naturalization were his three paper gods. My father bought his paper name to enter America, surrendered it to stay in the country, and refused to relinquish both names when he naturalized. Maybe my father is a new species of tree in the Flowery Kingdom.

After he confessed, paper was his god. As his fear of deportation grew, he kept every sheet of paper with both his paper and blood names.

I kept paper too. I still have two letters that he wrote me. He used the simplest characters because he was unsure how much I'd retained from Chinese school; the characters distilled his message to its potent concentrate, a calligraphic tonic. Each letter, no more than a handful of characters, had a clear directive.

During Mom's first round of chemo, when Dad "sojourned" in Houston, he sent me a letter.

"Come get me," my father wrote in his boldly penned square characters.

But it was the postcard of two surfers in Hawaii, in the wild ocean near Hilo, that showed me who he was as a father, as a man. I was living in Berkeley, and beginning to write my first stories. He sent it to our family home in San Francisco, addressed only to my name.

The message: "*Yuen leung*. I can't be at home."

"Home." It can be translated to mean the place where a family lives. If I believed this translation, it meant his abandonment was about a street, a ghetto named Chinatown.

"Home." It can also be translated to mean family. This painful, intimate translation meant our father was giving up on us.

Yuen leung. My father intimated its meaning so that I understood: *yuen* means "willing," which implies original intention. *Leung* means "compassion."

Today I am older now than he was when he wrote this note, and I realize what it must have taken for him to ask for pardon. In our family culture, forgiveness is never an option, so we didn't have a word for it. I now know: my father was asking for a generosity of heart, for trust in his love. I can hear him intone: *"Disregard the outcome of my actions and trust my original intention."*

I kept the card and whenever I read it, I become his child again, hopeless to help him. He'd had a hard life, and I'd had a lifetime of cultivating a plan to relieve him of suffering.

Even today, what moves me is his signature. He didn't sign with the formal "Father." Instead he used his paper name—the fake American name—as if his abandonment were also fake.

10

OM NEVER smoked, so when her stage IV lung cancer was diagnosed in 2001, I knew it was from working with the phthalate-laced polyester in the sweatshops. Just as heat from the body releases formaldehyde in polyester mattresses, the cancer opened her storehouse of fury: at the mother who sent her into marriage, at the husband who robbed her of hope. She had a quarter of her metastasized lobe removed and started chemo. The brothers told me Dad tried to help, walking close, doing Mom's bidding, but she refused him at each turn. Everything he did was wrong, everything he touched was ruined. Every time she saw him, she saw her cancer.

From New York, I talked to Dad and he was resigned. "Your mother needs a place to deposit her fury." So, when Aunt Juvenda called, he agreed to go to Houston to stay with her and her husband. I told him they needed help in the burger bar.

It was like musical father. That he let us bounce him around from house to house, toss him from relative to relative, made me sad. But what was the alternative? How dissimilar is this from other post-Exclusion marriages? It was a time bomb. He'd get bored, then furious, and then I'd go get him and Wendy would have to take him in. Exclusion teaches us to always have a backup plan.

After forty days—the length of a sea voyage—even my sister lost patience. Luckily, I happened to be with my guy, Ner, in the high desert outside Los Angeles, and he offered to have Dad stay with us. He told me that getting to Irvine meant going through the most brutal of LA traffic, so we had to leave early, get Dad, and then get right back on the road.

My sister mentioned a quick sister-chat and so when Ner made good time getting to Orange County, I was happy. Taking care of Mom, I hadn't seen Wendy in person for a few years. It was Ner's first time meeting Dad and Mr. Lowe, Wendy's father-in-law; Ner was worried about being alone with two Chinese-speaking fathers, but Mr. Lowe spoke excellent English and had come to Wendy's to say goodbye to Dad. I waved to the men. "Be back soon!"

Wendy took me to South Coast Plaza and let me have my espresso before telling me why she wanted to meet.

"Dad was upset," she said. "He cried."

I let her tell me what she wanted.

My sister repeated his words: "Sixty years I've been here. Sixty years I've worked, and I have nothing."

I didn't want to ask how she responded.

Wendy told me, "I hugged him."

Whereas I chatter, using a thousand words to create confusion, Wendy's a tai chi grand master who doesn't waste a breath. She waits for the right moment. And I was speechless when she unexpectedly posed a question. She didn't ask, *Why did they marry?* She asked, *Why did they have us?*

I just sat there. My sister has a confidence I don't have with our parents. As the second born, her powers of observation are finely tuned. Her quiet isn't fear, it's timing. She got up suddenly. "We better go back. Poor Ner's been alone with both dads."

* *

Wendy was only three but clearly remembers Mom's face after discovering Great-Grandfather's body. Mrs. Yee was with her and watching the store while Mom went to deliver lunch to him.

My sister told me how Mom rushed into the store, as if still running away from what she had just seen. To this day, Wendy can still hear Mom's long, shuddering scream.

Great-Grandfather lived in the storage room of our grocery store until the health department evicted him. After that, Mom made and delivered meals to him at the San Fran Hotel. She kept his lunch favorites in rotation: preserved duck eggs, pork with shrimp paste, tripe. On weekends, I accompanied her. Great-Grandfather's room was on the third floor, at the end of the hallway with a view of Coit Tower.

On that awful day, Mom went alone. She would tell us how she knocked and knocked while balancing a tureen of soup and a square tin of the rice and vegetables in one hand, how she called out but there was still no answer, so she retreated down the dark stairwell.

The manager barely looked up from his newspaper. "He's probably asleep."

"Open the door for me," Mom said.

Manager Lee slipped the keys through the barred window, but Mom didn't want to touch the tangle of metal—dirty green and blue brass—and insisted he come along and open it for her. The request for a kindness quickly became a plea for pity. He snapped his suspenders back over his shoulder. "So much trouble."

Grabbing his ring of keys, he stepped into the lobby like a warlord and locked the office. Heading up the stairs, he grumbled as if Mom had committed a crime. With each step, she offered him gratitude. *Manager Lee is a kind man. Manager Lee is a good man.*

I knew those stairs. The dark was deeper than our garbage alley. There was an odor, and the carpet was sticky.

Great-Grandfather had had an operation, but the pain-killers either had not arrived or did not work. Maybe our Old One didn't understand Western medicine or the

understanding wasn't translated. Details that even if accom-
plished may not have mattered. He was ninety-two. What
desperation he chose not to bear we can never know. He had
the determination to coil the sheets into a rope, the perse-
verance to get the rope to hang from the frame, the will to
slip the noose around his neck, to pull up his legs, to let
his weight gather and snap his breath, choking him out of
his life. Who can manage that kind of plan at any age? Our
Old One was not afraid to walk the road, and we have all
been given this by blood.

Later that night, when Dad came home from his job at
Bethlehem Steel, Mom's eyes darted back and forth as she
told him what happened. I remember looking at my father's
face for an answer, Mom's face was too hard to look at.
Dad told me that her *om*—her courage to face life—was
almost gone.

As they made plans for the funeral, Dad also made his
plan to get to Hong Kong. I was with him when he tipped
the dispatcher at the union so that his name would float to
the top.

At Great-Grandfather's funeral, I was the only child in
attendance. After we walked the processional, Dad took
me aside and told me a shift in the engine room had come
up—the worst assignment—and that he was leaving in the
morning for Hong Kong to get medicine for Mom. "You
are in charge, take care of your sister and brother."

When the ship docked in Kowloon, Dad had less than two hours onshore to accomplish what he had come to do. Luckily, his cabbie knew the wet market and deposited him with the most esteemed snake master. After Dad told his story, the snake master agreed, "Death disturbed your wife's spirit, snake gall will restore her courage."

Dad followed him into a room with a wall that was lined with rows of cabinets, each one with a narrow door that was only barely larger than an airmail envelope. The snake master unlatched one and the door fell flat forward to reveal a resting snake, its greenish body no thicker than his wrist. He woke the serpent, coaxed it onto his arm, and then gripped its head and squeezed below its neck till the forked tongue darted out. Then he hammered a nail through its skull and just as quickly drew a razor down its entire length to extract a small dark orb, which he handed to Dad.

"Consume one now, in common feeling for your wife. This will begin to steady her."

The snake master selected five more serpents, nailed them onto long boards, and gutted them. Dad said their long bodies glistened like strands of dark Tahitian pearls. The snake master slipped the five gallbladders into a long, thin vial, filled it with alcohol, and said, *"May Guan Yin protect your journey."*

The cab got Dad back to the harbor just as the ship's horns were blasting the last long blow. He scaled up the side of the vessel, the rope ladder swinging wildly; the captain cursed down at him.

Go to hell, Dad thought. In his pocket, he had the five snake galls and, in his heart, hope was beating.

* *

The night Dad came home, I stayed up after my sister and brother went to bed. When Dad showed the vial to Mom, she asked how much it cost, but he didn't answer. He told me to get a soup spoon and I brought the porcelain one with the fish that Mom liked. I watched Dad carefully pour out the alcohol till a single gall slipped out. Mom said it was like a frog lung. Then he lit a match and held it under the spoon.

I watched as Mom gently swallowed. Then her tears came.

"*Om.*" Dad told her she already had courage. The snake gall was only replenishment.

* *

We were back on the road after picking up Dad from Wendy's in Irvine. After Ner got through the most aggressive of traffic on the 405, we coasted on our short stretch of the I-5. It was twilight, and the water of the aqueduct cascaded blue and orange, a Ferris wheel of light. I pointed it out to Dad, who was already smiling.

Ner gave Dad a quick smile before saying to me, "Your father understands English."

"It's temperamental," I said, "like his hearing."

"Right after you and your sister left, Mr. Lowe started telling me about opium." Ner was stunned because Mr. Lowe was elegant and mannered. Ner asked, "Would he tell this to just anyone? Is it my long hair?"

I shrugged (maybe because you're "not-Chinese").

Ner described the scene that unfolded between the fathers at the dinner table after Wendy and I had left for South Coast Plaza. "Your father was sitting slightly behind Mr. Lowe, enough so that Mr. Lowe couldn't see what your dad was doing, but I did, and your dad knew it. Mr. Lowe was telling me about opium, that it was given to mourners to relieve their sorrow. And suddenly your dad became Charlie Chaplin, jabbing forks into two dinner rolls and walking them across the dinner table, all while looking right at me. There was a bamboo flute in the middle of the table, and your dad pulled it toward him, then reached for a teacup and placed that alongside the flute, pantomiming smoking an opium pipe."

Ner said, "I could practically see the oil lamp heating the opium." He continued, "Meanwhile, Mr. Lowe was telling me about why opium is healing. He said, 'It puts the body at rest so it can heal itself.'

"Your dad is hep," Ner insisted. "The way he tilted the cup, he knew opium was smoked on your side, on your hip."

By this point in Ner's recounting of the opium story, we'd made it to the 14. And like everyone, Ner was speeding like crazy.

"The Scholar and the Outlaw," Ner continued, "one knew about it; the other had the complete experience."

After our exit, a long dirt road led us past a boutique farm with a buffalo, a longhorn steer, and a few potbellied pigs, which entertained Dad. Then we were driving up to the house and Dad was fascinated with a row of ocotillo, the thorn-ridden shrubs planted along both sides of the hill. I could almost hear him wondering, *Where are we?*

Ner's driveway was lined with two rows of giant golden barrels. The Jag barely came to a stop before Dad jumped out, ran past the barrels to the large boxing glove cactus, gathered a handful of fallen prickly pups, and brought them to Ner.

I translated. "He's rescuing them."

This surprised Ner, maybe more than the opium. But now Dad had cactus thorns all over his fingers.

We went into the house, where Ner took Dad into the kitchen and turned on the strongest lamp, the one we used especially for this purpose. With a magnifying glass and tweezers, he plucked out most of the microscopic prickles from my father's hands. When Dad pulled his hand out from under the hot lamp, he saluted Ner. We showed him the house and midway through, Dad leaned in and whispered, "His father must really love him. He bought his son such a big house!"

I didn't tell him that Ner bought it himself.

When I showed Dad his bedroom, he took one look at the size of the California king, threw back his head, and laughed. "Big enough for two wives!"

The air was thin at three thousand feet above sea level, so I let Dad sleep in. Late morning, when I went in to check, I marveled at the sight of him in repose, his hand a soft fist under his chin.

*　*

Years later, when I'm sitting with our father's body in the family home, I remember what he told me in the desert house. We have three spirits: one that lived in the body, one that went on to the netherworld, and one that lived on in the ancestral tablets erected in our home.

11

WENTWORTH ALLEY, 1963.
          I'm the only child and Mom is the only
          woman in attendance for Great-Grandfather's
wake. We're in the back room of the vegetable store. I see
the cap of a snow pea under my chair.

Dad had wanted the three of us to send Great-Grandfather
off, but Mom said that baby Antony was too young and
Wendy too scared.

"First girl Fae is six, old enough," Mom said.

"I'm five," I said.

When Mom reminds me that my life before birth counts
as my first year, I feel proud.

Dad goes to open the store for a few hours before the
service. After breakfast, I take my brother and sister to Mrs.
Yee's and then help Mom gather the incense, funeral papers,
the white and red envelopes for coins and candy.

I'm wearing the new wool coat Mom made, but the wet
wind is sharp on my face. We walk quickly down Pacific,

along Dupont, and then onto Washington. At the park, we turn onto Wentworth Alley. At the end of the block, we go into a store and enter a dark room.

Two Orphan Bachelors are sitting at the back. They're wearing pale armbands on the sleeves of their jackets. I sit on a chair at the edge of the row and watch Dad help Mom put on her mourning robes. I've never seen her so still, like the porcelain Guan Yin that sits above our icebox. Mom raises her arms and Dad drapes two long, pale panels of muslin along either side of her. He ties a thick black sash to her middle. Dad puts another sheet over her head and folds the top to make a point, then pulls the front down low so the hood hides her eyes.

Mom's wailing scares me, but I don't cry.

She chants the names of Great-Grandfather's two sons and daughter in Hong Kong and I feel them float in like ether. When Mom throws herself to the ground, Dad catches her.

Sitting on three wooden blocks, the coffin is long because Great-Grandfather was a tall man. I can almost see the top of his slanted forehead and feel him peering at me over the ledge of the pine box.

Near the coffin, Grocer Kee urges a fire to roar out of a large metal can, the orange and blue flames flicker like tigers' tongues. He slips rectangles of paper into the can. One strip escapes and floats toward me, but he warns me not to touch the money for the dead.

Mom shows me how to clasp my hands over my chest, to bow deeply from my center. "Earth," she points at the foot of the coffin, and then at the front, "Heaven."

I think about the many times I walked Great-Grandfather down the steps from the back of our store where he lived to the front of the store where he watched for shoplifters. My job was to make sure he didn't fall. I took tiny steps and stopped; he took shuffling steps and stopped too. When he sat down on his wicker chair, he reached into his pockets, pulling out a roll of Life Savers. I loved watching him peel away the frayed silver edges to expose the colored disks. Then he smiled from behind his whiskers. "What will be your favorite color today?"

After the three Orphan Bachelors pay their respects, the coffin is closed. Dad and the others lift and carry the coffin out of the building. At the doorway, Mom hands out strips of ash-white papers to the Orphan Bachelors.

As we step outside, Mom pulls me into a vestibule and says, "Quickly, lift up your shirt."

She rubs the thick funeral papers over the rash on my belly. All night I'd scratched and then woke up with the T-shirt stuck to my skin. I cried as Dad used oil to tease away the shirt. In the open air, the rash spreads like two red continents across my stomach and the cold gives the rash a green tinge.

"Listen to me." Mom's voice is urgent as she instructs me to repeat what she is about to say.

"Dear Old One: Today as you leave us, take this child's illness far away with you."

No words come out because I'm feeling embarrassed to speak to the dead and all I can do is push my face into my mother's skirt. I believe that my rash is a map of my mother's deep anxieties: a newborn, two girls under five, a mother and sister in Hong Kong to support, an incompatible husband. I am sickly. I have asthma, severe eczema, and bad eyesight, conditions none of my siblings suffer from, ailments that my parents don't trust Western doctors to treat. Mom has her cures. For a fever, she boils an egg, unpeels it, and slips a dime deep into its warm center and rolls it back and forth over my forehead till the egg cools. If the dime comes out blackened, the fever is extracted. For stomach aches, she boils Coca-Cola, one of the few times I am allowed soda. For headaches, she heats knobs of ginger over the fire, wraps them in a small towel, and rubs it over my temples. After Lunar New Year, after the pomelo dried up, Mom had me bathe in its thick rinds to relieve my itchy skin.

But my large patch of rash wasn't something she could cure with a potion or poultice and we went to the Jackson Street Apothecary to see Dr. Woo. I put my wrist on a tiny velvet pillow and waited while he found my pulse and listened to all my organs. I stuck out my tongue so he could examine its color; he smelled my breath. He asked Mom about my appetite and which foods I favored, and then he prescribed a medicinal tea of dried crickets, slabs of herbs, tree bark, and bug shells. Beginning that night and for the following weeks, Mom brewed the tea till it was a thick, muddy sludge and then she double brewed it to make sure every ounce of healing was extracted from the dregs. It took at least an hour to consume, with only three fat California raisins to chase away the potent aftertaste. But it wasn't this bitter brew that cured me. It was Great-Grandfather who took my ailment away to the land of the dead.

* *

Outside, the Orphan Bachelors are lined along the alley like soldiers. Mom hands them each a white envelope with a coin of sorrow, and I hand them a red envelope with a Life Saver candy. Sweetness chasing sadness. Hurrying after the hearse, we throw our funeral papers as if casting white tears.

"Great-Grandfather is leaving." Mom tells me to wave, and I do. She continues in a low voice, pleading to Great-Grandfather. "The ills you must take, the good fortune you must bestow from afar."

I button my coat and stand there, my eye on the hearse that takes Great-Grandfather away.

12

SUMMER OF LOVE in Chinatown, San Francisco. My father was on a navy supply vessel to Vietnam; my mother was minding our grocery store near North Beach, the nerve center of the Summer of Love. I was just ten and this was not my summer of love. Even though North Beach with Yone Beads was just down the block and City Lights Bookstore only around the corner, I had no time for peace or patchouli love-ins, be-here-nows, or tripping on Monterey Purple. I was too busy for Hare Krishna-ing around with flowers in my hair. We were setting up the store. And we were settling down: my job was to tutor Mom for her naturalization test. It was our summer of work.

When my parents got the store, there was a lifting in their spirits, a camaraderie taking hold. Mom and Dad turned decisions over and over again, considerate of the opposing view, patient with the other's worry. Every choice was a conquering of fear. When Mom came up with the idea of calling the store Kim Hing, the name of Dad's ancestral village, he beamed, not only with pride but also with love.

To make the sign, my father broke off a box top and etched out the shadow letters K-I-M H-I-N-G in reverse. Making a stencil and then using a razor blade, he cut out the prototype. After he spray-painted the name onto the window, my sister and I stood back to admire his calligraphic flair. His confident lettering, so significant to witness, a man without English writing such beautiful English. He hadn't asked me to help with the spelling, so it was a revelation and a wonder how all the words that belonged to him were always right, however he spelled or wrote it. I remember how proudly I stood with my sister in front of the store, the sun on us, the name Kim Hing a flying kite across the large window.

We kept the store as Old Man Jue had it so that when he came to visit, he felt like it was still his. There's a fuzzy black-and-white photo of my sister and me standing in front of the center aisle. She's clutching a coloring book and I have my arms around her; we are beaming. Behind us, the large, belly-shaped jars stand as tall as my toddler sister. They're filled with dried herbs, almond seeds, persimmons, and dates. Also on a shelf are boxes of preserved mustard, pickled ginger, dried shrimp and scallops, salted cod, cured duck, and ropes of lap cheong sausages. The expensive boxes of ginseng, coils of bird nests, tangles of seaweed, and black mushrooms are kept behind the counter. Chef Boyardee and Campbell's Soup were stacked on the shelf by the front door, along with the Vienna sausage and Spam. In the back was a freezer with ice cream for children. At the counter, we had nickel bags of shoestring potato sticks, senbei crackers, and dried cuttlefish, alongside exercise books, ink brushes, and slabs of ink for Chinese school.

After we closed the store, we shopped for dinner. I learned to squeeze hairy melons to test their maturity, bend snow peas for snap. I copied how Mom slit her thumbnail into the white stalks of bok choy to judge its crunch. At Hop Sing's, I tucked myself in between the space where the two refrigerator cases met in a triangle and watched the butchers flirt with my mother. At the chicken store, she asked for a red-haired hen (actually brown), and when it was brought out flapping, I learned to check that its beak wasn't chipped, its eyes not cloudy, and its legs not broken.

For dinner Mom made a soup, steamed the chicken with long beans; we ate quickly and then I washed the dishes and swept the kitchen while Mom bathed Antony. At eight, Night Boss Chan dropped off several bundles of precut fabrics. That summer, smiley face T-shirts were in demand.

My mother would untie the hazy purple bundles and lay out the parts: shirt front, shirt back, two sleeves, and a crew collar. I helped stack the parts in their sewing order. Then we took it to the machine. The Singer was like the dark head of a stallion, and it was loud. My sister was sleeping not more than two feet away on the Murphy bed.

"Do like this." Mom matched up the shirt front with the shirt back. "Pinch the seams together and hand it to me by its bottom edge." She slipped it under the sewing foot and I heard the needle punching and eat-stitching all the way through the long seam.

I nodded; I wanted to help. I matched up the seams and held it level to her working hands. She stepped on the pedal and pumped. Mom pushed the fabric under the sewing needle and leaned forward. Her neck tightened, her back bent. Mom was the workhorse in yoke and harness charging out into the paddock—I was her stable girl, crimping, prepping, and racing after her.

All twelve smiley faces flew like Laffing Sal over the machine's edge. Mom's arms flew up and then came down with a yank and she sewed the opposite seams. She worked so fast the shirts became linked like prayer flags, then it was my job to snip the umbilical threads that joined them.

One dozen smiling T-shirts. A penny a seam, two cents for each collar, three cents per sleeve. One dollar. Eight cents. I tied up the bundles and stacked them by the door for Morning Boss Chan.

But this was not our only work. While Mom sewed long flowing dresses for the flower children, she also studied the naturalization questions. My mother became an American as she dressed a generation of rabble-rousers.

I spread out the hundred questions typed on onionskin paper over the clean kitchen table and then pointed out the ones that I, too, was studying in my social studies class.

Our windows were open and we heard guitars strumming, and happy hippie chatter drifted into our apartment. The air bloomed with night jasmine opening on the vines and time simmered, sweetened with incense. I watched Mom slow into a moment of contentment.

First, we worked on her crib sheet. I read each question slowly as she repeated the sounds and then wrote out its careful, aural equivalent in Chinese characters above the English alphabet.

Old Woo, the clerk at Chong's Suppliers, taught Mom how to transliterate English words into Chinese characters and then to sing out her order.

Nai been keem (you become Aunt) was "napkins."

Gum bao sui pei (gold precious water fart) was "Campbell's Soup."

Ma see low moon (horse shit road smell) was "mushroom."

Then she told me how she said goodbye. *See yow doe mo lorh* (soy sauce don't have) was "See you tomorrow!"

Mom didn't have time to learn English, so she made time by not wasting time. As comfort and counsel, she recalled what her mother had taught her: "The sun is our gold, but once its needle moves into shade, time is lost forever."

I'd pick out five naturalization questions and repeat them till she had them memorized. Sometimes she'd finish sewing her bundles before she learned the questions and answers. The next day, she'd study those five questions while running the store and that night, I'd review the old five and teach her a new five.

One afternoon, we got stuck on the word "about." I couldn't explain why it was important. Finally, Mom thought of it as Ah-Bao, the name of a dog. "*Precious Dog*," she said, giving the word a human weight.

Our Summer of Love was *about* Mom becoming an American.

After Mom learned ten questions, I quizzed her. After twenty-five, it was a test. After fifty, it was an examination. I stood behind her and in my most rounded American accent, barked questions at the back of her head.

"What are the first three words of the Constitution?"

Wey dai pei bow (hey big butt treasure) "We, the people."

* *

As summer heated up, fashion went afire: pirate shirts, Nehru tunics, flowing paisley frocks, hip-huggers, and culottes. Mom always made her morning deadline and always made my sister and me mini versions of the flower-power garb: a Sgt. Pepper jacket, hot-pink hot pants, a pair of striped double-wide bell-bottoms. She hung each outfit above the frame of the Murphy bed so that it was the first thing I saw when I opened my eyes.

During the day, flower children came into the store for the nickel bags of snacks. When a teary-eyed pregnant girl showed up, Mom went to the back and brought her a bowl of fried rice. Hippies felt betrayed by their families, by their country, and were forming communes outside the traditional definition of family. But we, we were doing the opposite: Mom was loyal to the concept of family: she wanted to remake the family that had been destroyed by the Chinese Exclusion Act. She wanted to reunite with her mother and become a daughter again.

No matter that thank you/excuse me/I don't know was all of the English she knew. Mom wouldn't let anything deter her. She taught me that language was power, devotion wordless.

As a child, I looked at my mother's back more than into her face. When I discovered Tillie Olsen's *As I Stand Here Ironing*, I understood I could write about labor as love. When my mother sewed, I felt her devotion to her own mother, this fearlessness she put to achieving her dreams, it, too, was a rebellion going on that summer. My mother taught me there are infinite ways to make a revolution, that sacrifice serves the story. She taught me that the rebel had to be fearless toward the dream.

I am still the daughter standing behind my mother's sewing chair. I know the intimate contours of my mother's skull, the soft points on her ears, the dip of her lobes, the round of her back, and the protrusion of her shoulder blade. I see her strong back, feel her fierce gaze, hear the bare gasp from behind her pressed lips, and smell her scent as her hands and feet dance cloth to life.

Mom took the naturalization test and passed. She was sworn in just before Thanksgiving.

13

I N China, when Grandmah negotiated her daughter's marriage contract, she wanted the groom to sign a promissory note.

"I give you my daughter. Give me your word that you'll reunite mother and daughter in America."

Dad refused to sign. "What I say, I do." His belief was to create—he had a word for it but I can't remember clearly, but I still understood its meaning and intent—a togetherness of feeling, a skill at getting along, a willingness to build one heart with many rooms of sympathy. That was the business of love.

In America, he kept his word. He entered the Chinese Confession Program and swore that his name, You Thin Toy, was fictitious. His citizenship was revoked. His bride did not consider his humiliation. He swore injustice and their marriage soured. He accused her of using him. She forbade him to continue. "Wanting my mother with me is no betrayal."

Dad went to sea and Mom managed the store alone. She put my sister into the baby carriage, and we walked to Chong's Supplies, which was at the far edge of Chinatown. I helped her stack supplies into the back of the stroller and I carried a pack of napkins, sometimes a stack of paper bags.

There were many late nights when she cried. Our neighbors, Luday and her husband, spent many evenings consoling Mom. From my eavesdropping and finding their letters, I've pieced a story together. Great-Grandfather was old; my sister and I were too young to help. She wanted him to stop going to sea, to find work on land.

Recently I found a letter she wrote to my father in English. Her penmanship shows she has not started to learn the language. Her letters are unbalanced, the top and bottom of each alphabet stiff, as if she wanted to add more strokes, as if a kingdom lies in wait behind each letter, ready for an uprising.

Finding this note meant my father kept it and brought it home from Yokohama.

Four English words: Baby Sick Come Home.

Each word is capitalized as if they were singular characters, almost like soldiers each sent out to do a job. I knew this letter was quickly cobbled by Luday's husband, a Chinatown waiter. The letter wasn't written for Dad but for the captain who had the power to let our father come home. I know there was a more intimate letter in Chinese, but I haven't found it. Perhaps I stopped looking after I found the aerogramme where Mom tells of her first pregnancy: "My body has happiness."

* *

Four years after the Summer of Love, after Mom studied, learned, and then forgot her naturalization English, Grandmah arrived. Mom was a seventeen-year-old bride when she left her mother and now she was forty-three and had given birth to four children.

The reunion at the airport was pained. I watched my mother's anxious eyes fall on each passenger who departed the customs door. When Grandmah came through, I saw an old woman with a harshly threaded widow's hairline, in dark tunic and trousers. She wasn't the vibrant, protective mother my mother had described.

Mother and daughter were strangers with no boat of hope. I wasn't surprised when three days later, they fought and Grandmah said, "Your enduring-heart is at the bottom of the sea."

The ocean of peace that had separated them became their ocean of bitterness.

* *

When our mother arrived in 1953, the first thing she wanted to do was to find her grandfather. Dad took her to the Square and he showed the tea label with her grandfather's name to the chess players, who directed them to the benches at the edge where old men sat in their dark suits. My mother approached each man until a whiskered face turned up at the calling of his name. He nodded as if he'd been waiting for her his whole life.

My mother said, "I am your granddaughter."

My father watched and saw a doubling of love. The Old One smiled, the weight of his patience, his sixty years of waiting lifted. He saw his wife smile too, to find kin was a rebirth.

* *

When Grandmah arrived in 1971, the first thing she wanted to do was go to the cemetery and pay respects to the father she'd never met. We all helped prepare the feast for the dead: a roast pig, a cooked whole fish, and a steamed whole chicken. Everything had to be intact, head and feet, wings, beak, snout, and tail. Each sentient being had to be offered whole, a gesture of our piety. My sister and I collected joss sticks and counted out the hell notes for Great-Grandfather to use in the netherworld's commissary. The brothers picked out thin-skinned oranges and they also brought firecrackers. We piled into our station wagon and drove our "picnic" to the Chinese cemetery in Colma.

We stood on the windy hill, watching our father try to keep the funeral papers and joss sticks lit. I watched Grandmah on her knees, bowing, her forehead touching the ground, her body folding at a perpendicular angle toward his tombstone. Three times, then three calls. The brothers ran around the cemetery firing off sparklers and rockets. My sister and I, unsure of how to feel, stood like stick figures and only nodded our necks forward three times. Upset, our mother called our bows shameful.

* *

We who were born in America have fixed birthdays, but Mom's birthday was always different because she used the lunar calendar; Dad's paper birth date was a secret best forgotten.

Since we missed Grandmah's sixtieth birthday, the one that celebrated the completion of her first cycle of life, Mom was saving and planning a seventieth birthday banquet party. I was surprised, because the cost of a banquet was not cheap. We children had been taught to not want. If we couldn't make it, we talked ourselves out of wanting it. We were also trained to share. Chinatown friends were shocked when I cut a peanut butter cup into four quarters.

Most families went to the teahouse on weekends, but we made our own dim sum. I would drizzle in boiling water as Mom kneaded the rice flour. While she rolled out the translucent dumpling skins, I made the filling, deveining shrimp, slicing bamboo shoots, carefully peeling the fresh water chestnuts, which were expensive. I'd chop everything all together and season it with ginger, soy, and cilantro. Sisters and brothers would knead, crimp, fill, and pleat the dumplings into purses of love.

Freshness in food extends life. Bok choy, water spinach, snow peas, and melons were driven in from the delta; live fish were brought in with freshwater tanks. A live chicken was selected and then brought home to slaughter. Freshly killed before it goes into the pot. Life gives life. At home, my sister and I stood at the sink washing chicken wings— plucking the stubborn hairs, scraping off the yellowed fat— till the wings glowed.

"No frozen food." Dad said, "No nutrition."

"No snacking." Mom insisted on set mealtimes so the body can rest.

Reading Marguerite Duras's *The Lover*, I laughed out loud. It wasn't the explorations into sexuality and colonialism and not even Tony Leung Ka-fai's stilted Cantonese dialogue, asking his father for one year with his lover in the 1992 film adaptation. It was that the narrator feigns pride: even though they ate garbage—crocodile—it was served to them.

We never ate garbage and we always served ourselves.

In Lao She's novel *Rickshaw Boy*, a poor man must eat for the strength to pull his rickshaw. The description of his hunger was the first time I'd read about the lusty first swallow of rice. When Dad came home from a long voyage, we all watched as he cradled his first bowl, how his chopsticks pushed the rice into his mouth, how his cheek muscles moved with vigor, and how he made gentle sucking sounds.

Years later, when my mother visited me in Rome, I found her playing with her fingers before bed and asked what she was doing.

"Counting the days since I've not had a bowl of rice."

The next night, we walked down the hill to Trastevere and I ordered her risotto with mushrooms and she was happy.

* *

For Grandmah's birthday celebration, Mom chose Tao Tao. I went with her to choose the dishes. After she ordered the main meal: chicken, duck, oysters, live shrimp, a steamed flounder, two types of greens, black mushrooms, and the roasted squab that was Grandmah's favorite, she paused on the soup: shark fin or bird's nest?

I thought about the shark. No matter which fin: dorsal, pectoral, or tail, the whole shark is sacrificed. It was the most expensive soup.

We always made shark fin soup for our seventh-day meal of the Lunar New Year. It was three long days of preparation. The first day was for boiling the fin till the odor was gone, during which the apartment smelled like a fish tank, the second day was for peeling the fine filament from the cartilage to get a bowl of translucent vermicelli threads and then boiling them till tender, and the last day was for making the many-bird broth. That day started early at 4 a.m., when the Mexican trucks with live birds arrived at Ross Alley. Because I was small, I went into the trucks, feeling quickly for the plumpest partridge (the breast) and the biggest quail (fills the hand). If there was a mountain pheasant, that was the best. Mom taught me how to grab them tightly under the cusps of their wings before jumping off the truck. They'd rattle in the paper bag as we walked to the chicken store for a Silkie, the black-boned chicken with its midnight meat that would give the broth its complex flavor. The rest of the day was spent slaughtering and plucking the birds; by evening, the rich broth infused the apartment, making us all crazy in anticipation.

Bird's nest soup, Mom's favorite, was only slightly less expensive. I liked the slurpy and chewy texture of the congealed bird saliva, which was good for our complexion. But like capturing shark fin, lives are lost. Thin men and young boys had to climb knobby bamboo ladders into high ceilings of limestone caves in Borneo. When the nests are captured, the baby swiftlets are destroyed.

My favorite was winter melon soup, slow cooked in its own shell, till the thick white melon meat fluffed up like cotton candy. The broth is savory from lean pork and spicy from the smoked Virginia ham and nutty from gingko nuts, lily bulbs, and almonds seeds. I liked how the giant melon, still green, was a garden on the table.

"Too common." Mom called the manager over.

I watched her tap her finger repeatedly at the menu as if she were trying to poke through the price.

The manager nodded. "No one will say you're not a filial daughter."

My mother snapped off each bill with a flick of her slender wrist. They fanned out on the high counter like Lotto tickets. She pocketed the receipt proudly and we walked out of Tao Tao like true patrons.

"That's a lot," I mumbled.

Mom made her puffing mom-sound, the one like she thinks I'm stupid.

"It's a lot of work to get to seventy."

Her voice sounded very loud.

Waiting for the light, she turned to me as if she were controlling traffic and then stroked my cheek more gently than I've ever felt. "I don't expect you to do this for me."

When my mother admired a dress, jacket, or coat, she'd hold the swing of the garment in her eye and take that image home and draw out the pattern on butcher paper, then onto fabric and she wouldn't sleep till the outfit was sewn and the fit was perfect.

As a widow, Grandmah had only worn the same dark uniform, so Mom wanted to sew her something magnificent for her birthday. First, she made a basted suit in an inexpensive cotton and Grandmah came over to be the model. Mom altered the jacket, gave it a stand-up collar to elongate her neck and slit pockets hidden along the side seam—functional and stylish. The skirt had a kick pleat that gave it an accent of easy movement; it fell smooth to the tops of her knees. Grandmah was smiling before she left to go back to her S.R.O.

I stayed up and helped Mom do the last alterations. I liked this time with Mom because she was relaxed, and we talked. That night, she told me that the banquet suit would be worn first as Grandmah's celebration garment and then later as her burial suit.

I kept making a face and Mom laughed. "If we were in China, we'd get her a coffin."

For the final draft of the banquet suit, Mom wanted to go to Britex, the fabric boutique downtown. Dad told me I was in charge, the tugboat that guided the vessel to safe harbor.

We walked there. In the Stockton Street Tunnel, the giant headlights of the delivery trucks revealed gasoline fumes as filmy as mosquito nets. As we exited the tunnel, the light felt thinner. Downtown people rushed just like us but they did it in straight lines, maybe because downtown wasn't as crowded as Chinatown. The women wore bright coats with swinging sleeves, their clicking footsteps sounded like an army of metal-tapping crickets.

The doors were just opening as we arrived. The big B was alone on one door and on the rest of the name, R-I-T-E-X, was crowded like all of us in our one-bedroom apartment.

We were excited and we were determined. As I walked through the first floor, I was mesmerized by the kaleidoscope of colors along the walls, the bundles standing upright like huge rows of Life Saver candies. I touched each bolt of chiffon, crepe, and silk. The second floor had stiff linens, slippery satins, and glassy-like moiré. On the third, the boucle, washed wools, and gabardine, and on the top floor, Mom found what she dreamed of: an emerald brocade woven with gold threads and embroidered with a flock of birds.

"Like phoenixes," she said, stroking the fabric as if to capture the treasured bird. When I heard the price per yard, my heart skipped. I didn't translate right away, then I saw Mom holding up her thumb and forefinger to make an OK circle. The clerk began to measure out the fabric and just as she reached for her scissors, Mom warned: "No cut bird."

Mom paid. Before she took the package, she smiled at the clerk. Then I heard her in a voice that was new to me. I felt her words like a gesture, I saw it as an obeisance.

"Thank you," Mom said to the woman.

Speechless till we got outside, I skipped ahead on Geary Boulevard, yelping. "Good job, Mom!"

The Stockton tunnel was packed and noisy with honking trucks, but my mind was buzzing. It wasn't the English that made me proud; it was that when she wants, Mom employs English.

There was no time to sew the suit until the Friday before the party. I stayed up to keep Mom company. I watched as she laid out the fabric, lining up the phoenixes so that their wings touched right above Grandmah's heart. Mom sewed the big seams of the jacket, the sleeves, and the collar. I ironed the collar and the pocket lining and all the interfacings. She finished the sleeves, sewed the long seams of the skirt, and when the suit held a life shape, she pressed the shell against her own body. In that moment, I believed my mother would live forever.

14

WHEN MY aunt Juvenda tried to teach me long division, my eight-year-old brain just couldn't comprehend the concepts. Exasperated, she started chanting the "Ballad of Mulan."

My heart was afire. What was this?

It begins, *Jik jik fook jik jik*. Mulan is at her loom. Mulan is sighing.

Like most children in China, Juvenda had learned "Ballad" by rote memorization. The staccato incantation stunned me. I heard the swooshing of the heddle slipping through the thick folds of the tapestry. The wooden pedals pumped; the harness lifted and dropped like an exhalation of worry. I heard the mechanics of weaving, the paddling back and forth that is Mulan's lament. Especially striking in our dialect, *jik* sounds like a thrust, an attack.

I also heard the sound of my mother's sewing. Night after night, more than twelve years of long, hard nights, Mom sewed into the darkness. My sister and I fell asleep to the needle whizzing and then we woke to the *jik jik jik* of her machine, our mother already spinning a sun to open up a new day.

Weaving, Mulan sighs.

"Why?" her parents ask.

"Father's name is on every decree," Mulan cries. The khan has commanded each family to donate a son to fight against the invaders. "Father's too old and Brother's too young, but each family must sacrifice a son."

Determined to take her father's place in battle, Mulan speeds to the eastern market to buy a horse, to the western market for a saddle and stirrups, to the southern market for a strong rein, and from the northern market, she picks out the longest whip.

Begone math! I wanted to learn the "Ballad."

This poem ignited my own devotion to my parents. They had come to this country with nothing, no horse or bridle, no rein or whip, and no long, sharp sword. They came only with their desire to fight and conquer and capture the best life.

And so, I spent one of my undergraduate years at UC Davis studying textiles. I wanted to learn to weave, to design and silk-screen fabric, to hire my mother and her gaggle of sewing lady friends and go into business. Weaving, designing, and silk-screening were fun but not enough. I returned to Cal, changed my major to English, and started writing stories about my parents' lives in the barbarian's language they never learned.

* *

During the pandemic, I teach a course on fathers and daughters in Asian American literature. For our last meeting, I assign the "Ballad of Mulan" in the original Chinese along with the Yenching Institute's translation by Arthur Waley. Many speak or at least understand their ancestral language, and several speak none. Nearly all of them have watched the animated Disney film of Mulan and, despite the mainland's lockdown on democracy in Hong Kong, saw the newly released live-action film.

"When was the last time your parents helped you with homework?" I ask.

Everyone looks stunned.

"Let's imagine. Your immigrant parents think their child at Cal no longer needs them. But one day the child comes back with homework that the parent knows, the 'Ballad,' learned countries and years ago, and they start chanting, *Jik jik fook jik jik*, and the child is speechless."

I know that unique blend of pride and shame. I ask them to remember the folktales their parents and grandparents told them, the ones that only required listening. "Go home and ask them to retell their Mulan story. Listen."

At our next class, their responses surprise me. Annie's father had bragged endlessly about Cantonese being the true language for poetry, but she'd never believed it till he recited the ballad for her. She was shocked when her sullen father transformed into an exuberant, confident man, a word warrior. He finished the last stanza with its long melodious sigh and then winked. "Bet your mom didn't learn this in Taiwan."

"I almost loved him then," Annie confesses.

I tell her what I learned from Teacher Owyang, that when poetry is recited in Cantonese, the rhymes are brighter because the tones have retained the sounds of ancient Chinese.

Michelle recites the opening lines of the "Ballad" and tells us that her mother had taught it to her. I note how she seems to take two breaths before shifting into Cantonese and also that she has the famed opera star Bak Sheut-sin's elocution, her eyes lit up. She'd been on the waiting list and when I told her that I never take anyone from the waiting list, she'd insisted. She made Asian American studies her minor and I had to let her in. In class, she's the first to hand in assignments and the one always asking for clarification, which translates to, "what will get me an A."

"I cast a wide net," I tell her. "Figure out what you want to give me and we'll both be happy."

"When I speak Canto, I want to be perfect," she says.

I tell my students what I discovered when I first heard the "Ballad," that work sounds can be art, that a woman's work can be noble, and how the staccato sounds of the first line inspired me to study textiles and then to write.

I ask if they know that the original "Ballad of Mulan" was written in the Northern Wei dynasty in AD 400, maybe even first by the Xiongnu in AD 300, that Mulan was a barbarian from China's northeast province, and in the Tang dynasty, 960–1279, the "Ballad" was rewritten, with Mulan recast as a Han Chinese.

What do they think of that? After we discuss the ownership of a story and whether history can be rewritten, we talk about translation. Where is truth written? In the original, the revision, or in its translation?

At our last class, my farewell is a recording of my aunt Juvenda's recitation of the "Ballad of Mulan." I tell them to shut off the video on Zoom so they can focus on listening.

"I want you to hear what I heard," I say.

They wait. The house is cold, and my fingers struggle to activate the Start button. Finally, it comes on and my aunt's voice sings out.

We listen.

When the screen goes dark again, we've run over class time, but it feels as if our time is infinite. One by one, eighteen bright faces pop back on the gallery screen like stars and I realize, as I always do at the end of a semester, I will truly miss each one of them.

Last night, while preparing for class, I finally picked up a square of paper that had been floating around my desk, that I'd been ignoring for years. To my shock, it was the "Ballad of

Mulan," all 360 characters of a daughter's devotion, written in my father's hand, his once-bold calligraphy wobbly from dementia.

Alone in the dark quiet, I held the "Ballad," will and testament that his hope lives on.

15

O
UR CHINATOWN apartment had two prized books.
The first, my mother brought with her from China.
A Lazy Girl's Wish is about a girl who doesn't want
to do any chores. Suddenly, the bed makes itself; a towel
scrubs her face. The pot of rice boils and the ax chops the
firewood; the kindling marches into the fireplace. The girl
is happy and then rebellion! The bed throws her off before
she wakes, the towel scratches her face, the rice burns. The ax
chases her all over the courtyard and when she jumps onto a
swing, it throws her off. The girl sits on the ground crying
and realizes that laziness is a trap. Even at nine, I knew it
was an overworked mom story.

The other book, *Eat a Bowl of Tea*, is Louis Chu's novel
about New York City's Orphan Bachelor society. It was
published in 1961, the year I started kindergarten, when I
was just learning English. It would take a decade for me to
find it. After I'd graduated from reading books for free at
the Chinatown Branch Library to sneak-reading them along

the curving aisles of City Lights, I would discover Chu's defiant, subversive novel. I didn't just read it. I inhaled it.

Two Orphan Bachelor fathers in 1960s Manhattan have been separated from their wives for decades and each has an unmarried child, Ben Loy in New York and Mei Oi in China. Playing matchmaker, the fathers send the son to China, where the overjoyed mothers stage a meeting. Ben Loy's smitten; Mei Oi's besotted. They have the traditional ceremony with a live groom instead of a live rooster. Their marriage is consummated. But after they leave the village and return to America, the union follows the pattern of all post-Exclusion marriages: it becomes sexless and doomed.

Only Mei Oi gets laid. Mei (for "America") and Oi (for "love") evokes American lovemaking. Honeymoon sex hooks Mei Oi and she craves it. Remorseful for the whoring marathons during his bachelorhood, Ben Loy becomes impotent, while Mei Oi's sexuality explodes into a compulsion. She hungers for sex and becomes consumed with getting it. She's a temptress, a sexual adventurer, a devourer of carnal pleasure.

Mei Oi is our erotic avenger against Exclusion. She demands sex as retribution for the childless wives left in China's empty marital beds and also the Orphan Bachelors living sexless lives in America. She wants to give life to make up for the wasted life of the silent film actress Anna May Wong, who is not only passed over for the Chinese lead in Pearl S. Buck's *The Good Earth*, but offered the role of the doomed slave girl who must commit suicide. Mei Oi wants to claim honor for James Wong Howe, the innovative cinematographer of the thirties whose marriage to writer Sanora Babb, an ex-lover of Ellison and unrequited love of Saroyan, wasn't legally recognized till the repeal of Exclusion in 1942, and they couldn't live together as man and wife till the repeal of California's miscegenation law in 1948.

In what may be literature's most comical seduction, when Mei Oi succumbs to the Chinatown sleaze Ah Song, her subversive aim is not just pleasure but motherhood. But if Ah Song's seduction is ridiculous, having his ear chopped off by Mei Oi's father is uproarious. It adds insult to injury for the pitiful fate of all Orphan Bachelors; Ah Song's only function was to be the seed dispenser. He is Mei Oi's gateway screw.

The birth control pill has just been released and America is on the verge of the sexual revolution. By 1962, over 1.2 million women will enjoy a powerful sexual liberation and Mei Oi becomes Chinese America's free-loving flower child. After a fortnight of not hearing from her lover, she eyes her husband's best friend and flirts shamelessly and mercilessly with him. Mei Oi craves the intimate touch, demands sexual attention, and lusts for its rapture. She claims America by procreating.

Get laid, get pregnant, get power. Mei Oi's womb is her gold.

What astonished me about the novel was how loud it was. Louis Chu gave life to my Toishanese. I heard the dialect of the hundreds of thousands that came from my homeland in Canton: the hatchetspeak of my great-grandfather working the abandoned gold mines; the seething courtesy of my great-uncle, a houseboy in San Antonio who later lost his business in the Watts riots; the gutter-hissing of army uncles, cousins, and brothers; and the blasphemous cussing of my merchant seaman father.

Toishanese is shouted, not spoken. Their speakers are loud, not only because they are fearless but also because they're uninhibited and *baa-bai*; everything is their business. Grandmothers shout from the front of the bus to the back as if in the rice fields and a typhoon were approaching.

Move! Move! Get out of my way!

Their curiosity was boundless and they demanded to know: *Did your husband sleep with that co-wife again?*

Louis Chu was the first to bring the richness of Toishanese to the literary page, to show death-cursing as crucial to the Orphan Bachelor society's fearlessness. If they held no power, they would holler and curse; volume warded off superstition and tricked ill luck. Chu made language the armor against sorrow. In the novel, the old bachelors met every situation with a death-curse. Go die! Dead beggar.

There's cadence, depth, and mirth: No can do. Go sell your ass. Sonavabitchee. Many-mouthed bird. Wearing a big hat? Pulling a big gun!

Its aim is as heavy and direct as a cleaver: the playboy Ah Song is described as a "three ply smoothie boy."

There's imaginative action: Talking toilet news! Boiling telephone jook!

Eat a Bowl of Tea was the only book I packed for New York. Maybe like my father's Book of Lies, I wanted to carry something personal to my new home. When I shared it with my new friends, a Hong Kong–born, European-trained oboist, a conductor from Shanghai, a painter from Hangzhou, and a fourth-generation Chinese American whose politically elite family had been immune from the effects of Exclusion, every one of them was baffled and then horrified.

Wow your mother. Stinky corpse. Fart drum. Sell your butthole.

"Why all these old men, and why this vulgarity?" Each scornfully claimed that this wasn't Chinese culture.

"It's Chinese America." I insisted that their class upbringing and East Coast squareness made them delicate.

"Wow your mother!" one shot back.

I smiled. "You got it."

✼ ✼

A Lazy Girl's Wish gave me the daring to want more. Even if I'm a workaholic, I still want what the Orphan Bachelors wanted: to *taan sai gaai*—luxuriate in time—to idle through my day or, in the parlance of California, to shoot the breeze.

Even if my training is: Why do one thing when you can do three? I just want to be the laziest girl in the world.

16

EARLY DECEMBER in New York City was a shock. It wasn't just the grime on the subway or that it was so cold I had to walk through Macy's to shelter from the wind or that my first apartment on Thirty-Fourth and Broadway had windows taped with large sheets of plastic. It was that New York was instantly home. I knew I could finish the novel that was impossible to write in San Francisco.

I loved the frankness in Manhattan, the take-me-give-me-show-me-and-take-no-shit attitude of seven million packed into twenty-four square miles. Artists filled the city with fever and abandon and I was part of the charge. Everything had a vicious grit; everyone had a surreal glam. Basquiat stayed several nights at my friend Barbara's Lower East Side storefront jewelry studio. Madonna in her pudgy glory stayed one night, and Annie Lennox too. It was a time when anything could happen. It was 1981.

Finally I felt some reprieve from the constant chaos, the never-ending need to worry about Mom and Dad. I still got the calls, but I couldn't drop everything and go there. "There" was three thousand safe air miles away.

So, I bartended lunch near Rockefeller Center, watching businessmen down martinis and ogle the arriving girls from the People's Republic. Many had no clue they were being fetishized and I'd stop explaining it because it seemed that after Mao, nothing was intolerable. For a while, after that shift, I headed farther uptown to hostess at Danny K's but, not being accommodatingly Chinese-y enough, I was fired. The manager did it in Cantonese. "I don't think this work suits you."

I was annoyed at his indirectness. Why didn't he just say: *You're a lousy hostess.*

Well, who wants a coolie-job? I'd written the series of letters that formed the narrative about an immigrant woman's journey to America, which had been developed at Sundance and was now being filmed in Manhattan. Mei Wah Chao, the location scout, became a friend and introduced me to Moira Dryer, who had come from Nova Scotia to paint. We became, as Mei Wah called us, quick-cook friends, like ramen. Moira was finishing up at the School of Visual Arts, breaking plates for Julian Schnabel and making stage sets for the avant-garde theater Mabou Mines.

From a fifth-floor walk-up on East Eleventh where Moira lived and then all the way crosstown to the Perry Street penthouse where she died, the city housed and grew our love. We explored the city, walking everywhere. After discovering the

Cloisters, we walked back to her place in the West Village. We walked the Brooklyn Bridge to BAM. Once, we walked the circumference of Manhattan. Well-matched scavengers, we combed through flea markets and thrift stores, finding the best stash before the secondhand smell seeped into our hair. On Wooster, in a turquoise slip dress, Moira climbed into a dumpster and tilted a door over the edge. Laughing, I caught the splintery edge, and this would be my desk—doorknob intact—as I worked on my novel.

We were young. We were women who worked hard, women who wanted some fun. Romance was a thrill, love could be a drug, but as artists, we wanted romance to be replenishment, the diversion that would charge up our work. Men could be trouble. Most didn't understand, couldn't tolerate or want to abide our devotion to our work. Moira said they just couldn't keep up. She didn't want a man to sit across the room and gaze adoringly at her. "What a horse weight," she scoffed. I wanted a man who knew when to get out of my sight so I could work.

I was called ruthless, self-absorbed, and hotheaded. Moira was mercurial and icy. Smitten male painters invited themselves to her studio and then, blinded with desire and cranky with competitiveness, offered vicious commentary. After one suitor's condescending remark about her muted colors, she admonished him sharply: "You don't like my work. I don't like you."

Moira dared to love her work first. But then she wasn't given much of a choice. She'd lost her mother to suicide before she was six and then her husband, Victor, to congenital heart disease in their first year of marriage. He'd gone out for a jog and then gone missing—for three days because he wasn't carrying identification. Victor was twenty-seven.

Moira's art defied her sorrow.

New York City was a writing dream upon which I'd built a relationship with another writer. I always thought of writing as a kind of struggle in which I needed a comrade. I came to New York first and six months later, my boyfriend followed. What I learned was that my devotion was to writing and his was to brooding. Living with him was worse than the family I escaped. When I described the poison of his darkness, Moira said, "Put up a sign on your door: KNOCK AND YOU'RE DEAD."

Moira blew everything up with whimsy. Eating Cheerios was eating air. When a chest of drawers made for her old apartment didn't fit into the new one, she switched on her saw and made it fit. A futon was king in the morning, queen by noon, and then forever after, it was the Big Waffle. As easily, she redesigned a dress sleeve from full and flared to fitted and sheer. Eating at a Mexican place on Fourteenth Street, I watched her trace the scallop ridges of a placemat and later saw it as the border of a wall-sized painting, *Damage and Desire, Damage and Desire*. My hair became the tone of one painting; the tire tracks along a beach on Boca Grande became the texture of another. Her mathematician aunt's flowcharts translated into the depth and sheen of *Deep Sleep*.

One day, Moira led me through Chinatown as she shopped for a stage set project—was it for Sting? Since leaving my Chinatown back west, I'd avoided Manhattan's. I had no contacts, no negotiation skills, and after we spent a few hours wandering around being treated like tourists, she suggested roast duck.

I made a face. "So bad for you, so fatty." But I followed her through packed Mott Street to Big Wong. Walking in, she waved to the fattest of the frontline guys, the smiley one with the giant tweezers, plucking half-singed hairs off the duck butts. Her favorite waiter came with tea, barking hello, already knowing her order. The food arrived minutes later, and Moira showed me how to scrape the fatty layer off the skin with a fork, popping the wafer into her mouth. "All the crunch without the fat, a duck chip," she smiled.

I felt as if Moira delivered me back home. As I took my first spoonful of jook, I told her how my mother brewed tiny jars of it in clay pots, our homemade baby food. Mouth Always Open had been my nickname because my mother saw that I'd inherited her hunger. She'd spent her childhood running from the invading Japanese, then the retreating nationalists, and then Mao's advancing army. Good guy, bad guy, every guy hungry.

Moira's mandate: don't let a man mess up the business of your art. My brooding boyfriend became my brooding husband. I'd naively thought that writing would save us, but it only doomed us.

For him, everything was insurmountable; he was noise sensitive, odor averse, light sensitive, always had a headache or a gut ache, was allergic to the pollen in spring, the sun in summer, the cold in winter, and to work, work, work. Lazy bubble boy.

He was all *annoying-hei*. There wasn't a day that I didn't want to strangle him. I should have known when he introduced me to his Augusta-raised mother, whose hello was: "There used to be a law against this."

Knowing all that, why did I marry him? Why didn't Mom's marriage teach me not to waste time with *endurance-hei*.

Long story made easy. He was "not-Chinese," so I was "disowned." Mom refused to talk to me for over a year. Then she decided to learn English so she could talk to him. One day they were alone, and she told him: "I love all my children, but I love my daughters more. They do more."

That he came and told me this has borne out the whole worth of that dreary union.

* *

Late one Saturday, he went out alone to get the early edition of the Sunday *Times*; after he handed it to me, he stood in the doorway. When I looked up, he announced, "I will always love you."

I felt his anger. "Are you going somewhere?"

He marched off, slamming the bedroom door. After a while, I put down the *Book Review* and got up to check. There, in just the next room, he overdosed.

A pair of Brooklyn cops arrived and eyed the apartment suspiciously.

"You sure have a lot of books," one said. The other remarked on the syringe that I had hanging from the kitchen window. He nodded slowly as I explained that it was our ailing cat's saline treatment.

I got the husband to the hospital, got his stomach pumped, then got him packed and took him to JFK. I sent him home to his mother, whose gleeful welcoming word was: "Finally."

In my mind, I called Moira, and I heard her say, "It's Mother's Day. Let her have him."

My mother didn't need to know, so I didn't tell her about the divorce till the papers were signed. Our family culture: take care of it; don't bother anyone with your small-stories. In the meantime, Mom was calling my sister every week to ask, "Have you spoken to the husband?"

"Fae's probably locked him in the basement," Wendy said and then she called to tell me she was sick of hearing about it.

Mom taught us: patience is a waste.

* *

Moira was twenty-eight the winter her cancer arrived. Chemo was treacherous, so nourishment and comfort became the project, and often it was jook that she craved. I got in good with the guys at Big Wong, called in my order, then jumped in my car and drove across the Brooklyn Bridge, pulling up to Mott Street. Big Wong was outside waiting and when he slipped that sun-yellow bag onto the front seat, the car filled with perfume and heat. When I got to Moira's, the congee was at the perfect temperature. She'd throw a magazine across the room. "Have a *Vogue* place mat."

When Moira wanted to see an herbalist, I called my mother for contacts, and she called third-tier paper relations in New York, who then called blood cousins. *How clannish*, I thought. But there it was: I had an introduction to the best herbalist, I would be treated like family.

When I unfolded the first square packet for Moira, she was entranced. Like two girls on a playground, we laid out each bug shell, every twig, each barky sheet, chalky slab, odd-shaped nut, every beetle and cricket skeleton. Moira wanted to know what each thing was, what they promised. But I didn't know, so I called Mom again. As she explained the medicinal properties, it got complicated. I got agitated and then upset. "Tell me what the herbs mean," I shouted. "I want to know what they do," I demanded.

My mother's quiet was a calm tonic. I felt her breath and mine followed. My diaphragm bloomed and then I started sobbing. I was her child, afraid now. Mom's voice became clear and she said, "Peace. Embrace."

Comfort. That was the only medicine.

I brewed the first batch of the healing tea and served it to Moira in her favorite celadon mug, repeating what Mom had said. "*On-wei.*"

Moira was quiet for a while. Then she said, "That sounds like one way."

We inhaled the tree-twiggy breeziness that now infused the room.

Moira worked hard but she played harder. It was her recipe for replenishment. In the two years she was granted a reprieve from cancer, she made fun her priority, visiting Deià in Spain, where she and her late husband, Victor, spent summers, and Boca Grande, Toronto, and Prince Edward Island to see family. When she asked for books, I took *Love Medicine* by Louise Erdrich off my shelf and *Rich in Love* by Josephine Humphreys. Moira said *Housekeeping* by Marilynne Robinson was her favorite. "This is my family."

The cancer came back. But Moira wanted to keep painting and when she didn't have chemo, she went to her studio and worked. In Chinatown, I got her a bunny hat, one that matched her blondness. Every day, Moira put on dark glasses, her late mother's seal coat, her Walkman blasted zydeco and she braved the burlesque-filled walk along Forty-Second Street to her studio on the East River.

Her family wanted to take her back to Canada. Moira said no. She wanted to die near her artist friends, in the city where she made her art. Barbara and I took turns staying over.

The cancer slammed through Moira like an escaped fire. Even then, she wanted to paint so we rearranged her apartment. She had worktables in every room, chasing the changing light of the long summer days. The unbearable heat permeated her work: *Having a Hate Wave*, *Sex Hex*, and *Poison*. These were about violence: the violence of the heat, the violence on her body, the violence of love.

Moira prepared me. One day she said, "I don't have much time."

When the advance readers' copy of my novel was ready, I brought it to her at St. Vincent's. She got mad at the nurse for putting gauze on it, saying sharply, "Get that off Fae's book."

I kept thinking, *She's still thirty-four.*

Moira's last night, she asked me to replace the hospice nurse. She woke once and told me, "Victor's waiting at the elevator."

I felt her passing like a blade of light shooting out the top of my head. At dawn, I left her apartment and started walking. This was how my mother taught me to walk behind the coffins of our Orphan Bachelors, taking the body on a last visit to their favored spots before burial. Buoyed by exhaustion, I kept walking east. I walked past the apartment she shared with Victor and then past her last studio on Varick. I walked with her defiance. I walked with her fearlessness. Then I was under the Manhattan Bridge and then I was in Chinatown and then I was standing inside Big Wong.

When I got home, I went straight into the kitchen, laid out the food on the counter, foil tin next to plastic tub. And then I ate. I ate to feed my friend. I ate the duck with my fingers, bit into the dark, rich breast. I sucked the crispy joint on the wing, the aged soy on the drum. I spooned mouthful after mouthful of jook into my mouth. The textures were crisp, moist, and juicy. I ate, urgent to feed the body and for the ritual farewell.

17

My mother taught me to never suffer a man's woes. Going to sea was becoming harder as he aged, even for a man who was used to hard work. Fuming became my father's job. When my mother got fed up with his seething against America, his hollering against Mao—all his grumbling pontifications—she sent him far away, off to me in New York City, where I was struggling to live and write and be young in a city teeming with hope, back then.

He'd stay until we couldn't stand each other—around forty days, the length of a sea journey to Asia. Until he got bored, he was easy to be with, content to do whatever I was doing. I took him to art openings, movie premieres, late dinners with writer friends, once to the Princeton home of a good friend who, after picking us up from the bus station, greeted my father respectfully before rolling her eyes and mumbling to me, "I can't believe you brought your Chinatown father to our apple-picking party."

Once, Moira was visiting and Dad made us cucumber sandwiches. He trimmed the bread and sliced the cucumber, then layered the thin circles inside the rectangle. He presented them to us as if we were first-class cruise passengers, he waltzed around the room, his raised hand swirling an imaginary platter back and forth above his head in swooping arcs. I translated: "The tables are nailed to the floor. If you hold the platter stiff over your head, you can't control the tilt."

Moira lay on the couch laughing.

"You have to let the platter swoop and glide, you have to undulate with the ocean," Dad said.

She said the sandwich was the cutest thing she'd seen all day.

Often, my father and I were invited to Mei Wah's, who lived in a fourth-floor walk-up on East Eleventh. Her doorbell never worked and I'd shout her name until she threw down the keys so we could let ourselves in. Sometimes the party upstairs was so raucous, I'd have to call from the phone booth in front of Veniero's.

Dad mused, "Visiting someone in New York is a lot of work."

Susan Agee, another friend, said that in a room filled with painters, writers, and musicians, Dad was the true artist, because while everyone drank and snacked, chatted and flirted, Dad was completely engaged, pondering every object in the room.

A filmmaker and a composer, now household names, were frequent guests. Before the composer became famous for his operas and movie scores, he was a Chinatown dishwasher. The filmmaker spent so long on his script, his wife unplugged and then removed all the televisions from the house. No more distractions.

One of Dad's hobbies had been to make Chinese flutes out of metal pipes and he brought one as a gift to Mei Wah. The flute was passed from guest to guest and when the composer played a Hunanese folksong, I saw that my father was a hit. Not a Chinatown laborer, not an illiterate waiter, but an eccentric, artistic soul—he fit right in.

Another night, I took my father to an art opening. He was proud of the American President Lines logo on his paint-stained coveralls and refused to change. So, there we were on Madison Avenue, among a sea of Manhattanites in black, my father stood out. Noting Dad's outfit, a man approaches to ask if he's a painter.

Dad understands enough English to nod. "I can do."

Ner's father, Jack Wesley, was one of my first friends when I came to the city. His work had a surrealist bent and the show that night included several of his Dagwood and Blondie paintings, a series of flat pink-and-blue canvases depicting the suburban couple in various poses of marital discord. There's a painting of Blondie sobbing on the bed, her flouncy dress hiked up, her naked bottom the center of the painting. Dagwood's arms are outstretched, desperately beseeching Blondie to stop crying.

Dad nodded in fellowship with the harangued husband.

Later in the evening, I find Dad smiling in front of *Night Titanic*, a huge wall-sized painting, black hull of the vessel charging into the foreground of the dark night, curlicues of waves rippling along the bottom frame. Five pink portholes smiling on the upper right.

Jack joins us. Dad begins talking, his English is as choppy as the rough sea in the painting, he's telling the story about the eight Chinese sailors on the *Titanic*, that they were leaving England with plans to transfer in New York and then to sail onward to Cuba. How two made it to a lifeboat but were trampled to death. Another man is found floating on wreckage, and this survivor would become the inspiration for the blockbuster film. The six surviving Chinese seamen were rescued and then delivered to Ellis Island. It was 1912 and Exclusion was in full force.

My father tells what happens to the six rescued Chinese men. "All deport."

Like those eight sailors on board the *Titanic*, my father, too, possessed an instinct derived from living with the rhythm of the ocean; he, too, would have sensed the peril that struck the vessel like a final exhalation underfoot. He, too, would have known to escape.

As I looked at the two fathers standing in front of *Night Titanic*, I understood what my mother tried to impart about giving life. A man has nothing in their physical being that makes fathering instinctual. A woman has her body to trust, life gives life. A father cannot call forth from his body, so he must—with magnificence—give his child courage in life.

18

M y brother Tim bequeathed more than his exotics. Besides the pair of cherry trees, there's a staghorn fern, a bird of paradise, a plumeria, several peony plants, and a purple rosebush. The plumeria wasn't happy so I dug up the root and sent it to Wendy's mother-in-law in San Gabriel Valley. It has now tripled in size and bloomed, the petals dried and enjoyed in tea. The peonies went to Maryland, where winters have a sustained cold, long enough for the plant to go dormant. Last spring, Maybelle sent a photograph of the magnificent hedge.

Tim also left me a crescent moon saber, named so for its moon-in-repose design. This heavy, six-foot wooden pole with its ten-inch-wide blade—one flat edge, the other curved like a resting moon, notched with spikes to catch the opponent's weapon—isn't your everyday sword. It's a Qing dynasty Manchurian weapon of choice.

Who could I possibly foist this on? This is during the pandemic when all classes are online. My students, of course!

Before class, I drag the saber next to a bookshelf, so they have something interesting to look at. Henry can't focus on our discussion and finally asks, "Where did you get the *guandao*, Professor Fae?"

I turn around and laugh. I'd forgotten that while clearing out the house, I'd used the wide, flat surface of the blade to collect the magnets I kept finding. The blade exhibits a collection: bumble bee, panda, butterflies, Mickey and Minnie, Tweety and Sylvester, and many varieties of sunflowers.

Ner had said, "You've emasculated the saber."

* *

It's fall 2019, before the Covid lockdown. We're in the last glorious flip of summer heat just before daylight saving time makes its switch, when the light drops like a blind, from sky blue at three to singe black at six. But that day, September 11 to be exact, the light is pouring gold, the sun burns, and the air is sticky at the crooks of my elbows. It breaks ninety degrees, so I send all my students outside to have a cocktail party without the cocktails. Practice for future soirees. I instruct them to ask interesting questions and give scintillating answers.

In the coolness inside, I do one-on-one meets.

Mia—born in Kyoto, raised in Princeton—is bilingual, bicultural, and bisexual. Her father does cancer research; her mother pines for Japan. Mia spends most of her time upside down, entertaining disabled children as a traveling clown.

Raymond tells me his mother sews in a sweatshop. He says it—no shame, no pride—just the fact, naked as if her work clothed her in respect.

"Hard work." As I say that, I realize that there are two children of sweatshop workers at the table. I add, "So did my mother."

He says he wants to work in emergency medicine, but that his mother doesn't want him to work that hard. I don't say it, but diligence is what he learned from her.

"I don't need a lot of money, just enough," he says.

How Chinatown. He was trained on what the elders needed; he is skilled at deflecting want. "Get what the others get," I say.

Jon is a Compton-born recovering addict with a father in prison for life. His eyes blink—defensive and vulnerable—as he refuses to answer one question after another. When I comment on his move to Covina, he is perturbed. "How do you know? Are you researching me?"

"You wrote it on your Q&A," I remind him. This is his last semester; he'll finish his memoir before leaving Cal.

The Violence and Business of Love is my regular fall class. We read novels about the complex hostility, absurd marital arrangements, Confucian manipulations, Christian disorders, and other maddening and loving contradictions that exist in so many Asian American families.

I call my students inside. Their chatter and laughter follow them into the bungalow; they've been building community, teaching each other.

Their sun-calmed eyes are on me. I ask: "Who knows the name Betty Ong?"

Every September 11, I give my Betty Ong assignment. An attendant on Flight 11, Betty Ong made the call to the American Airlines ground crew that led to the first-ever full closure of US airspace. I want them to listen to the last eight minutes of Betty Ong's life. It's an exercise in intimacy. The point is to listen to the recording alone and then again with a friend and then write up both the personal and the partnered experience.

In over a decade of giving this assignment, only Kelly Lam has raised her hand to say that she knows the name.

"Betty Ong worked Flight 11, the first plane to hit the North Tower." I tell them that her twenty-three-minute call to American Airlines alerted us to the hijacking, which led to the grounding of all flights and the declaration of a national emergency. I ask, "What would have happened if that call wasn't made?"

Then I reveal that Betty Ong was my classmate. "We were the tallest girls in the sixth grade, so we had to stand in the back row for school photos."

"This will break your heart, and this is the closest to a trigger alert you're going to get from me."

I tell my students that on 9/11, I was living in New York and I'd taken the subway downtown for an appointment. When I walked out onto Grand and Delancey, the first plane had just hit. I stood briefly with street bums and Wall Street suits, everyone insisting it must be an accident, the poor and rich were unified in this unfolding disaster. I kept going and got to my meeting. My accountant turned on his radio, but, still, no one knew what was happening. I thought about Kennedy. Only recently have my sister and I talked about it. She was no more than five, and at the store when people came running in to talk about the assassination of the president, and all she thought was, what does that have to do with me? That's the effect of Exclusion, not being entitled to feel like an American. I tell my students their generation is different, they're entitled to feel American, despite all.

Then the Campanile starts playing its catchy six o'clock medley, my students gather their things. I admire how softly their hands go in and out of their packs, how gently they depart as if in a processional. I watch them move into the fading amber light, their faces unsure but unafraid. I know now that this is taught—stillness, quietness, cousins of obedience and respect—in the face of suffering.

※ ※

Betty Ong and I went to the Jean Parker school. Those elementary school years are distilled in my memory as a dreamscape of hope, of young girlhood.

When her photograph was published in the *San Francisco Chronicle*, I recognized those eyes looking into the camera as the same ones in our class photo. Betty Ong was patient, unlike Robert Toy and Stanley Jue in the front row making faces and finger gestures. Betty held her gaze still. I accidentally glanced at my shoes, and that's how the photographer captured us. Recently, going through my late mother's papers, I found a newspaper clipping of me graduating nursery school at the Chinese Center; it's now been renamed the Betty Ann Ong Recreation Center. Mom prepared me: take the diploma, shake the principal's hand. In the faded newsprint photo, my eyes are caught, surprised.

We both grew up in grocery stores, so helping family was part of life. Like all Chinatown kids, she must have gone to Chinese school, too, but not to my Presbyterian one. Our Chinese names both have the ideogram "moon." Betty shared the same Aquarian birth date of February 5 with my brother Tim. She was my elder by ten months. In her family, she was the youngest. Neither of us would have children.

At George Washington High in the Outer Richmond, she grew three inches taller than me and would excel at basketball. I did not play any sport. Every day, we walked by the mural cycle *The Life of Washington* by the Russian émigré and Communist Victor Arnautoff. Recently, I asked friends what they remembered about those murals, and no one felt anything special. They were just there, in the entry wall, along the stairs: Washington and his slaves, the dead Native American. Maybe it also felt like a warning to us working-class kids of immigrants that we should stay in our place.

* *

After telling my Betty Ong story, I let class out. As I am crossing the Richmond Bridge, my phone starts pinging, my students reacting, my students rising. At home, I read their responses to Betty Ong like breaking news. When my students listened to the recording alone, the experience was like an echo tunnel, Betty Ong is trapped, Betty Ong can't escape, the terrorists have taken control. The cold ineptitude of the operator shocks everyone. Betty Ong is asked to spell her last name and identify her seat number at least three times. When she tells them that the cockpit is locked and that no one can get in, the operator says, "They're smart to lock themselves in."

My students listened a second time with a friend. I feel their hawk-eared listening, their want. They needed more from their chosen listeners. Mothers. Fathers. Sisters and brothers. Sisters cried with sisters; twins ran out of the room together.

"Betty Ong called her boss." I ask, "Who would you call, your boss or your mother?"

In unison, everyone shouts, "Mother! Mother!"

In Asia, parents protect their children. In America, children must protect their parents.

I've struggled to balance duty with desire, to do good by my parents but also to have my own life. What I can't teach and what education won't provide is the courage to put aside duty. I tell my students that they don't have to be obedient like their parents, the good Communists, or sacrificial like their grandparents, the good Confucians. In the sixteen weeks that I have my students, I expect them to put themselves first, to break the rules. I don't make it easy for them to succumb. I don't want them to become America's new artillery—doctors, technicians, engineers, and lawyers—the new coolies who will fuel this country's economy.

I give warning: daughters will always have it harder.

* *

Jeong Kwan, the Buddhist nun, has recently become well-known for her cooking, an honor gained without having a restaurant. She tends her own vegetable garden and cooks only for her fellow nuns and the occasional pilgrim to the Baegyangsa Temple near Seoul. She doesn't use garlic and onions because she doesn't want to increase libido, the deterrent to a calm mind.

At seventeen, Jeong Kwan left home with nothing and walked up to the Chunjinam Hermitage to become a nun. When her mother died suddenly, the pain was so great she decided never to have children, never to subject anyone to such suffering.

Teaching has given me the children I never wanted. Students enter my classroom never having heard about Exclusion or Confession, but before they exit, I teach them how both are still a weight on their sexuality.

* *

On my desk, I keep a small photograph of my mother. It was taken in 1947 and is a miniature stamp of her time as a teacher in rural China. She's wearing early Maoist garb: the pleated skirt, cinched belt, a crisp shirt, her hair freshly cut from braids to bob. Behind her is an open-air classroom: dirt floor, thatch roof, bamboo table. Her charges sit on low stools, their arms extended stiffly because they're wearing two or three padded jackets.

My mother is leaning over one of her students, who— either tired or hungry—has his head on his desk. He is sleeping. My mother has told me about this little boy, how she always had to wake him.

"Little friend, little friend," my mother would nudge him, "wake up and learn your lessons. Today we have a new word."

In the classroom, my mother is my inspiration. My goals as a teacher are many but most importantly this one: that none of my charges fall asleep.

II.

LANDING

My parents
with their
firstborn son

The sisters with
our parents

19

TIM'S TRUE loves were his creep of tortoises. The last thing I needed were exotic creatures that would outlive me by two generations—that brat. He had a guinea pig and hamster stage, a boa and python period, a bird stage with a coop of prize chickens, an amphibian phase with glowing toads and bearded dragons, and a slobbering big dog obsession. All this started at the Villa Rosa in Chinatown where we raised four Easter chicks to full-sized roosters and hens. The brothers played with them as pets before they became a course for dinner. There were also crayfish, live shrimp, crab, and tadpoles before they became frogs and even, gasp! two turtles. The slaughtering didn't go easy on the brothers. When Airplane, our favorite "red" chicken was killed, Tim sat on our rooftop—also our playground—sobbing while holding its long red tail feather, calling Mom a murderer. This was how we became American, not raising animals for food but raising them for love.

Tim's animals comforted him because he was no longer the youngest, the last one.

In the beginning, the torts reminded me of giant cockroaches with helmets, so I got rid of ten quickly. I drove a pair of Indian stars to Tim's friend in Hercules, three sulcatas went down south to Laguna Niguel, two red-foots to Millbrae, a gopher tortoise to Lodi, and a pair of desert tortoises to their homeland in the Mojave. Who knew torts were so popular?

I wanted to sell the last two and drove them to the Vivarium, emporium and expert on all things reptilian, but they wouldn't touch Dewdrop—an endangered Californian desert tortoise protected by law, a fugitive best to keep harboring—and Yang Guifei, the Amazonian red-foot, who was more beautiful but too common. Both were sneezing so I took them to the vet—an expensive mistake. They had upper respiratory infections and vitamin A deficiencies, so I learned to give them their antibiotics.

And so, my mother's tested truth came to pass, companionship gives rise to compassion. I was felled by love. First with the Amazonian beauty, the yellow dot on her head like a tiara, the curly flourishes along her cheeks like rouge, and the ruby splash under her mouth, her flirty charm. A row of vermilion spots run up her back legs like a pair of sexy stockings, even more endearing because of her fat ankles. She glides languidly and then pauses to look backward, so I name her Yang Guifei after the sulky imperial consort who ruined the Tang empire.

Dewdrop's beady eyes don't make her pretty. Her scrunchy face and jutting jaw give her a scowl; she looks pre-prehistoric. But she's got a lot of personality and is very attuned to her surroundings. She follows me around and is interested in everything I touch. When I vacuum, she's afoot; when I talk on the phone, her head bobs as if no one's listened to her for centuries. When she yawns, I'm taken aback by the wide pink tongue and her moist mouth. Her armor is a work of self-sufficiency, flat scales along the wide pad of her claws, long overlapping scales down her forearms, a chain mail of scales along her lower leg, and then a proliferation of spikes on her thigh, the protrusions pointy and sharpest near her tail, which itself is thick as the tip of a Phillips screwdriver.

Just under the rim of shell above her head, along the curve of her neck is a band of mottled skin. It is the most delicate epidermis. When I peer at her dark translucent shell, which glows green, each scute is a window that reveals the true color of blood before it meets air.

So here I am today, caretaker of these Taoist creatures, the true Orphan Bachelors, long living and miraculously adaptable. Dad once described the tortoise as the galaxy, their domed shell, heaven, their flat plastron, earth, and their life organs within, our immigrant souls.

Whenever I'm working too hard, the tortoises' rustling reminds me to put down my manuscript, go to their pen, and watch how they move with a different governance. Taking care of my brother's loves, I feel his deep loneliness.

* *

A desert tortoise needs fifteen hours of light and San Francisco isn't the Mojave, so Ner set up a UVB light timed to come on at dawn, which also gets me up.

Grades are due today. I make a pot of coffee and sort my students' finals into two piles: "boring" and "not boring." I've learned to start with the boring pile, no expectation, no aggravation.

Dewdrop is always the first to stir—before the geckos and before Yang Guifei—but I hear nothing, so I walk over to the pen. Yang Guifei looks up at me with her innocent, misty eyes. I push away the newspapers and find Dewdrop in a pool of blood, her serpentine head limp between her thick arms. It's a crime scene and there's blood everywhere.

"Dewdrop!" I call out.

There's no movement. She's no wider than my outstretched hand so I pick her up like a hamburger. Her shell and plastron are fine; I press my fingers into the cavities and feel her fleshy appendages. She has no cracks on her elephantine soles, and when I search her eyes for pain she only peers back with curiosity.

As I wave a nopal cactus pad, she starts coming toward me. Her left rear leg pops, her right front leg kicks, then she switches, right rear popping in sync with her kicking left front, three feet on the ground, one renegade foot always in midair. Up and down, a rock and a dip, tilting left, tilting right, cha-cha-cha. Even though the nip of her beak and her hot breath are reassuring, I wrap her in a towel and we go to the vet.

Berkeley Animal Hospital is packed. There's a mastiff, a parrot making car alarm sounds, and a bearded dragon with a chain fob on its leg. I pull out my stack of papers to grade.

"Dewdrop!" the receptionist calls out. I carry her into the exam room and set her on the shiny table. There are rows and rows of glass jars filled with cotton balls, tongue depressors, and superlong Q-tips. On the counter, tops and bottoms of shellacked tortoise shells are laid out like bikinis.

There's a knock and a man with a curved back comes in through the sliding door. His right shoe has a very thick sole. Dr. Harkowicz greets me and then announces, "Today is my first day back after heart valve replacement surgery."

I smile back. "Congratulations."

As I describe what happened, Dr. Harkowicz keeps his big hand over Dewdrop's pancake-shaped shell, and I see her relaxing onto her plastron. He taps along her spine, listening with his stethoscope, her lungs are clear. Then he presses his fingers under her shell to feel her organs. "Let's have an X-ray," he says.

The technician takes Dewdrop after telling me that it will cost $138. I'm shocked, but do I have a choice?

Back out in the waiting room, I pull out my stack of finals. After a decade of teaching, I take the first assignment and read the story twice, but I can't find its heartbeat. Teaching overwhelms me because I practically pay to teach these classes, so why am I doing it? For insurance. I can't die.

Who will take care of my creatures?

* *

For over a decade, my brother was very sick, first with Graves' disease, then with achalasia, an autoimmune disorder. "Achalasia" means failure to relax. Tim's esophageal muscles failed to open; eating and swallowing were excruciating. He'd described the debilitating pain, the roiling convulsions along his chest and abdominal wall. He told me, "It's the same muscle group used for birthing."

Severe pain made Tim difficult; the opiates changed him. Illness gave me a different brother and him an indifferent sister.

Cruelly, I'd called him an addict. Beneath my fear was impatience and beneath that intolerance was anger.

Truthfully, I was short on love.

Then, I was living in Berkeley to be closer to campus. A few times a week, I came to shop and take Dad to dinner. Wendy was in Los Angeles, and on her drive home from work, she called Tim. Dad was my charge, Tim was hers. But the more I took care of our father, the more Tim felt he wasn't cared for.

I never saw our parents nap or take to bed with a cold, so I lacked the patience for any physical discomfort. Our family did not respect pain. Everything was to be tolerated otherwise we were accused of being lazy, or worse, having *no-hei*—lacking courage.

"Try fighting off a bunch of drunk sailors," declared Dad. "Try running from the Japanese!" countered Mom.

Their competitiveness taught me that the one who had it worst was the hero. So, I wanted to be that last, most-pained person who conquers everything, a master at endurance. 100% *baa-bai* girl.

* *

The X-rays are done, and Dewdrop is called back into the exam room. The films are in the light box and Dr. Harkowicz outlines the perimeter of the gallstone. I'm not looking at where he points because I'm fascinated with Dewdrop's skeletal rendition. Her skull is a jade pendant and her armored arms as meaty as crab claws. Her head and extended limbs extend to make a five-point star.

Dr. Harkowicz continues, "Dewdrop's not processing her protein." He describes the operation, the yearlong rehabilitation, and the high danger of infection. "We gas her and then saw through her shell."

I say no. "What about the blood, where's that coming from?"

He shrugs and says with a skeptical expression, "Daily baths might dissolve the stone."

"I'll do that." I gather Dewdrop, go to pay, and then balk some more. "That's more than half my paycheck!"

The receptionist smiles. "Isn't Dewdrop worth it?"

"My own X-rays don't cost that much!" I grumble and demand a copy of the filmy X-ray. "I'm making art with it," I say.

Back home, I put Dewdrop into a warm bath and keep refilling her tub as I work on grades, which I get in minutes before midnight. I find Dewdrop asleep, her thick forearms over the tub, her honeydew eyes puffy from the soak.

* *

Valentine's Day 2015 was the last time I saw my brother. I was bringing food to Dad and got to the house just as Tim was leaving with his dog. So, there we were. I was a week late but I wished him a belated. It was his forty-ninth—the seventh year of his seventh cycle—the volatile time, Dad warned, but never explained.

Tim was a grown man who had worked in finance and made more money than any of us, but he'll always be the nine-year-old pipsqueak I took everywhere, to classes at Cal, readings and openings, and once to a Winston Tong performance where the artist changed his pants onstage. Tim had been wild with curiosity. "Why'd he do that?"

"It's art," I said.

When Tim was a baby, I carried him on my back with the same baby sling that Mom used to carry me and Wendy. That's how I took him to the park and on errands. No hands!

He adored me, but he also loved to annoy me.

When I invited him to Rome for my book launch, we got into a fight, so bad that I changed my seat to the opposite end of the plane. It was a long flight back to San Francisco and of course we bumped into each other waiting for the toilet.

That last time we saw each other, I was defensive. I was still holding a grudge about our last fight, not that I could remember what it was about. We were a family in constant battle. I was crabby and in family matters, *baa-bai* bossy. No time to ask or explain, only time to bark out my orders.

But that Valentine's Day, Tim was the large-hearted one. He gave me a hug and told me that he loved me. Following his lead, I hugged him back, then once more. I told him I loved him.

Not more than two weeks later, Tim was gone. I was making coffee and getting ready for my class when his friend Sharlene called; she'd let herself in to his flat and found him seven-days dead. My shock was complete. The cops had already been there, and the body was being transported to the county morgue.

But I needed to be where my brother had last been so I drove home. As I walked through Tim's flat, I felt calmed and decided that I would go teach my class as scheduled. As a writer, I had to face life, and as a teacher, I wanted to show my students how a writer lived. I told them that my baby brother had died, that it was sudden, that I was told he had not suffered. Then I confessed that we had been feuding, that we did not end well.

My students listened. Hearing myself tell the news altered my pain. I was showing my students that story began in witness. I was telling the pulse of my story. I was showing what it took to unfold truth. Suddenly, each student became dear to me; their listening made me acutely aware that I was entering sorrow.

* *

I was living in New York when Tim was having his complicated operations. We weren't close then. But one day, he called me before the most extreme one—requiring them to break his ribs in order to reconstruct his esophagus—and he told me, "If anything happens, I want to be with Mom."

"What's going on?" My tone had been distant, cold. I sounded bothered. Whatever I was protecting myself from is awful to remember now.

I may have listened, but my response was hard. "You'll be fine."

It's too late to change what I didn't do or to take back my callousness.

And then I buried Tim's ashes. By myself. I didn't invite my sister. Wendy had already flown up several weekends in a row; she and her husband, Nelson, had taken care of all the expenses, so I was being practical, not bothering her.

Our family rhythm: there was always too much to do. Each member had a job and each job had to be done without bothering others. In our family, work was work; work did not involve feelings.

When I texted my sister the time of Tim's burial, I thought she might want to know the moment of our brother's interment; I thought I was being thoughtful.

She texted back right away: "Does it have to be now?"

If not now, when? I knew our family's penchant for letting things pile up, I knew that if it wasn't taken care of now, she'd have to deal with his ashes—and maybe mine too— but I kept my mouth shut. I'd forgotten that being second born, she was used to watching and waiting, acting only when confident that her actions would be perfect. Being firstborn, quickness and efficiency were my training. Perfection was getting the job done.

When did I realize that my efficiency was also thoughtlessness?

Now I know the cost of my efficiency, that muscle I was trained to develop. In life, my impatience failed my brother.

In his death, my efficiency failed my sister. I disregarded that she, too, lost a brother. But she never made me feel bad, never suggested that my haste might have been a need to remove my guilt.

My sister's reply was measured and kind, which was befitting the word "elegant" in her Chinese name.

"I thought there was time for this. I would have come."

It didn't hit me till I got to the cemetery and the funeral director said, "Just you?"

But I had no time to fight, no time for hurt feelings. Tim had told me he wanted to be with Mom. Now he's the baby at her breast for eternity.

* *

Then our father passed.

Tim's death had been sudden, and though our father's had been expected, the two—a flash of lightning, a shock of thunder—hit like a forecast of greater damage.

The top floor of The Far East Café was already reserved. I decided to stick with the plan; I believe Dad would have insisted. Tim's Celebration of Life five days later was a balmy eighty, unusual for April. Friends and family members arrived as the bells tolled from Old St. Mary's Cathedral. The banquet room had a karaoke sound system, a stage, a disco ball, and a dance floor. We were a group of eighty. When I signaled for the food to be served, the manager gave me a look of disgust. I'd rejected the traditional bland meal for a funeral, choosing the sweet, crispy fare for a baby's first-month party. He'd explained that the comfort meal shouldn't be tasty, but I didn't want to eat sad boiled and blanched mourning fare. I wasn't letting Confucius ruin my brother's party. As the food was served, most of the crowd enjoyed it but I heard some of my mainland friends grumbling that they didn't have this tradition of feasting around death.

I told them that maybe this was our American invention. Our pioneer forefathers fled famine in China to become houseboys in America, to run chop suey joints, laundries, and fisheries. They developed the Bing cherry, the Meyer lemon, the early fruiting apple, and the cluster tomato. If the Orphan Bachelors were lonely in America, their left-behind wives were lonelier in China. Our ancestors were hungry for sex, starved for sustenance, and as their descendants, we inherited a profound, insatiable, and raging hunger.

Then I asked for stories, but respectfully shy—or shocked at death—all of Tim's friends were quiet.

"I'm the mean sister," I reminded them. "We've got three hours. Everybody speak up or I'm calling on you."

Matt stood up to mention Tim's generosity as a virtue and a fault. Sharlene said Tim was as talented at giving love as he was at receiving it.

During a lull, I told them about Tim's naming. We were nine (me), seven (Wendy), and three (Antony) when given the task of picking out our baby brother's American name. Somehow Oscar, Noland, and Timothy became the top contenders, so I wrote them on slips of paper and shook them out of a Junior Mints box.

After the Jell-O and almond cookies, coffee and tea were laid out, I thanked everyone and then told them that our brother was at rest with our mother. Then I announced that our father had passed, and that his burial was in the morning.

* *

The semester is finally over and I have a break. One afternoon, I hear whining sounds from the garden and find Dewdrop straining. I worry she's constipated until I see something underneath her shell, not her tail, but something long that extends at least half her own body length, enlarging and blooming like a sea anemone. It undulates. It's mesmerizing, the fleshy head is fluorescent and yawning.

I go back to the animal hospital with her-him. "You said Dewdrop was a girl."

"It's difficult to sex torts," Dr. Harkowicz says.

I rename him Mister Dewdrop. The days lengthen, the sun lingers over the large stones of the back garden, and my misgendered tort basks until the last of the sun leaves. One day I see him stomping on the still-warm stones, his member dragging behind him. Doesn't he know how to retract it?

Then, another crime scene; this time with penis fanfare! Again, blood is everywhere, on the walls, all over his shell, the squirting just won't stop. How much blood does he have?

I get close and then I see it, a notch on the blooming collar of his organ, blood is pulsating out in an arc.

Again, I call Dr. Harkowicz, who tells me, "Next time it happens, I'll cauterize or amputate."

I can't even think what to say to that. All I feel is Tim laughing, loud and mightily.

Falling in love with Tim's exotics doesn't salvage our falling-out, but it gives my brother back to me. It's not forgiving the pain but forgoing the grief that allows our love to return. I'm in a moment of succession—not a salve nor a trade—as I care for his creatures. This act allows me to ascend into his love. I do what my loved brother did for his loved ones. My hands become his hands and my care becomes his caring. And with this momentum, my love for my brother evolves.

Tortoises are one of the longest-living creatures on earth. They are master energy conservators and live by a different time count, seeing and seeing before easing into death. From them, I've learned how to meander, to have a temporal sense of luxuriating in time.

My mother needed me to "do more," while my father urged that I "do less." And now, these tortoises teach me that by doing less, I am doing more.

Taan sai gaai was Dad's guidance for the good life.

Tortoises manifest this quality of luxuriating in time. In the Shang dynasty, over two million years before Christ, the first writings were etched onto the shells of turtles and then burned; the cracks were read as divination by Taoist priests. My father had admired the mystery and wisdom of these giant sea creatures and when he saw the carapace in Papeete, he carried longevity home for his sons.

Mister Dewdrop and Yang Guifei have become my grand masters of the unhurried tempo, wandering through life, observant and carefree, moving with curious abandon. What they see is commensurate with the road they traverse. How they travel is with bold determination, dedicated resolve, and in a grand majestic saunter. Baudelaire wrote about the rebuilding of Paris during the reign of Napoleon III and describes the 1860s as a period when the flaneur comes into full glory.

Colette also wrote about the flaneur and flaneuse—the gentleman and lady strollers, idling, strolling, idling, exploring Parisian boulevards, inspired not only by the tortoises' meandrous pace but also by their all-consuming eyes. In the film *Colette*, a bejeweled tortoise makes an appearance in the salon.

My exotics—my flaneur and flaneuse—teach me that it's not my last moment with Tim that is the true count of our love. The true accounting is in the magnificent fan of our many, many moments.

Here I am, a woman who never wanted children, with charges that will live longer than any grandchild. When I find Yang Guifei's baby photos, I realize she's always been Tim's favorite. Even as a hatchling, she was pouting, demanding an emperor's attention. I figure that she's about thirteen, only a schoolgirl in her projected life span of seventy-five years.

From his endangered animal license, I know Mister Dewdrop is five and will easily make it to a full century. Along
with my literary trust, I've set up a pet trust to take care of
their psychological well-being and physical well-keeping.

Continue the love, I hear my brother saying.

* *

Many months later, the medical examiner called with the
toxicology report. "Your brother had a very, very big heart.
Over big." If Dr. Moffatt had said enlarged heart, cardio-
myopathy, or diseased heart, would I have been relieved?
Her tone was gently unhurried. Her information was clear,
and her directness said what was known—and what was
unknown. Her patience was not learned but as the Chinese
term calls talent, *heaven-birthed.* She let me ask and ask, her
answer always the same, but each time spoken with a longer
breath: "Your brother had a very big heart." I asked to hear it
again and again even if it made me sadder than I could bear.

* *

That last time I saw my father, I signed him into what would
be his fifth time in hospice. Anne, the nurse, was from Hong
Kong and her Cantonese enunciation was crystalline, crisp
consonants with the delicate curl at the edge of phrases that
made me think of those tragic Chinese heroines in movies.
When she gently addressed my father as Old One, I almost
burst into tears.

Before leaving, the caretaker, nurse, and I transported my father from his old bed to the new hospice bed. We folded a large bath towel and slipped it around his waist so that the ends were on opposite sides of his body and then we spread out the towel and used it like a swing to hoist him onto the other bed. All through this, my father was attentive and amused. He smiled and said, "Just like taking a piglet to sell at the market."

Bellowing, the caretaker corrected, "Not a piglet, but a very large, very old pig."

My father's rascal eyes twinkled as I kissed him. I drove back to Berkeley to teach my class.

Before dawn, my father departed onto the road. I let water lead me and drove the two bridges home. It was low tide over the Richmond Bridge and the trio of trees on the island shimmered like seals. The sky began opening as I drove the shoreline. San Quentin was lit up like an old man's birthday cake.

Water. Steel. Man. I felt the land rising to attention for my father's passage.

After San Rafael Bay, the road curved through Marin, rising along the evergreen line of Mount Tamalpais and flowing past the rolling hills of Sausalito. With the land stretching ahead and the earth moving underneath me, I thought of the world without my father. The sky brightened. I drove. In my heart, my father was swimming the clouds, soaring in the currents of wind and water. Approaching the Rainbow

Tunnel, I prepared myself to see his body. Inside the caterpillar passageway, I tooted the horn like Dad always did, his way of announcing, "Coming through, coming home!"

The surreal canvas on the other side of the tunnel always stuns me, but that day, the lines were magnificent: the wide blue sky falling into the water, the white sails of the boats pushing up toward the clouds, the redbrick pylons of the Golden Gate, a fire ablaze. This vista had captured my father's young heart. Now, these were my sacred waters and these golden pillars, my port of entry.

On the horizon, a large container ship guards the bay, a floating hell. I see the *Golden Venture;* I think about my father—the boy on the SS *Coolidge.*

I exit the Golden Gate and follow the foghorns home.

When my maternal great-grandmother died in China, my mother was not more than seven but knew to perform piety. She removed her shoes, loosened her hair, fell onto her knees, and crawled, wailing into the family home, calling the dead.

In obedience, I do the same. Then I sit with my father's body, I see that his mouth was set in the same childlike expression as when I'd brought him a bouquet of blooming dahlias, a taxidermy quail, or the found hummingbird nest—gifts I knew would please him as his health declined after the first stroke. Always shy about pleasure, my father feigned surprise. He was never direct with his feelings; he felt that was an impolite form of communication. He'd prefer to tell his caregiver, who might relay it to me. "Your father said," she'd intone, "if this daughter has something good, she brings it to her father."

"Deh," I whisper, bending to kiss my father's forehead. As my hand rests on his chest, the warm cascade of his blanket was a lingering of hope.

* *

Our father was among the last to be detained on Angel Island in 1940. He entered the Chinese Confession Program in 1966 and regained his citizenship through naturalization in 2001.

Depart. Our father's death date is April 27, 2015. In death, our father became an American. But I can still hear—and feel—his pronouncement: "Exclusion and Confession, the two slamming doors of America."

At his funeral, as the casket was lowered, my sister turned to me and said, "Dad waited."

My sister's love for him was the kindest of us all. She understood that he bestowed on his last son the chance to honor his father. Tim was the son who became the gentle spirit leading the Great One onto the radiant road. Through those narrowing margins of the disfavored, Tim's devotion forged a way to sail the straits.

20

OUR RANCOR had immigrant ingenuity.

What's wrong with this family?

My sister's been asking that a lot recently.

When Tim died, my friend Gretel was in town and helped me comb through the flat, looking for his will. After an hour, she stopped, hands deep into some files, and said, "You have another brother?"

Our mother's funeral was the last time the family saw Antony. That was March of 2003. Wendy waited, not calling Antony till late April and only to gently suggest, "Nothing special. Dad will be happy just going on your errands with the grandkids." When Antony didn't answer, she told him to think about it. "I'll call tomorrow."

The next day, his number was disconnected, and all his friends were instructed not to give the new number to his sisters.

"Are we witches?" Wendy demanded.

Year after year, the sisters flew in to do Dad's shopping, cooking, and cleaning. I was still living in New York and when Dad's toilet overflowed, it wasn't that hard finding a Chinese plumber to go over, but explaining it to Dad was really hard. He kept saying he could fix it, which translated to, he could live with it. When he needed a new stove, Wendy not only arranged to have one delivered, but also for Lily, her Chinese-speaking friend, to go over and explain how it worked. But when Dad started leaving the gas on all night and then getting lost going to the post office to pick up my mail, we flew out to San Francisco to arrange for a caregiver to come in every day.

Why didn't we call on the brothers? Tim lived upstairs and Antony was two blocks away. But the lines had been drawn at Mom's funeral. I don't know if the brothers believed that the only way to love Mom in memory was to keep her regrets alive. That caring for Dad was a betrayal? Who knows? Dad was alive and I couldn't just abandon him.

In our first-generation family, birth order overpowered everything. Sibling hierarchy had no rule or reason. I got my parents' first love, their relaxed and cozy care, so of course I owed more. Wendy arrived almost two years later, Antony in five, Tim in three. As the eldest, I was in charge. If my siblings made a mistake or got into trouble: my fault, my fault, my fault.

As the eldest at the Villa Rosa, I was also its unofficial babysitter. Taking care of children made loving children easy, and for a while I wanted to be a nurse.

Our Chinatown years had been our least contentious time because our parents' marriage had a unified purpose: the children must thrive. The sisters should be useful; the brothers shouldn't be useless.

We sisters were raised in Chinatown. Saturday fun was going to Big Uncle's poultry store and being useful was plucking chickens, ducks, and squabs. On weekdays we helped Mom at the sewing factory.

The brothers grew up in the Outer Richmond before it became the Second Chinatown. At home in the evening, they helped turn collars while watching TV (the sisters hadn't had TV); in the daytime, they rode bikes, explored China Beach, Baker Beach, and Mountain Lake Park. Chinese school was only on the weekends. In the summers, they went to camp. But what travails they endured as boys I never knew and never found time to ask.

When Dad was on land, he took us to Sears Roebuck and let us buy anything we wanted (Wendy and I shared one pair of skates, the brothers chose bikes, one each). We went to Playland at Ocean Beach, where the horse-sized Laffing Sal's canned laughter scared and fascinated us. When Antony did his maniacal imitation for Mom, who had stayed home to sew bell-bottoms, she laughed too.

In our tiny kitchen, shared with our four growing chickens, we made mini pizzas with saltine crackers, using ketchup before we knew how to make marinara sauce. The brothers stacked Cheerios on toothpicks. Wendy made cupcakes and let the frosting harden into chunky candy tops. When Dad was away at sea, Mom took us—two bus transfers and one streetcar—to Ocean Beach, the journey itself like going to the edge of the world. We were armed with fresh squeezed lemonade and dumplings and we refused to leave until the sun set. Our eyes trained on the horizon as Dad taught us, watching for that green flash just as the sun disappeared. Was that when each of us developed our love for the ocean, looking far into the horizon, looking for our father?

We played Holidays. Big Aunt's children gave us their silver-tipped Christmas tree; we dyed eggs and hunted them at Easter. Wendy and Tim used Mom's Singer to make Halloween outfits: Tim was a giant cockroach and Wendy a pretty dinosaur. They wanted me to be a huge can of Raid. I refused! On Thanksgiving, we went to Big Aunt's, and while the turkey was roasting and our second-generation Christian cousins played Twister and Monopoly, my sister and I were in the kitchen helping Big Aunt break up the fermented rice cakes to distill into Chinese liquor.

When Dad was a sailor at sea, he had the solitude he needed. Always a creator, Dad returned with ship-made creations: clocks, miniature fans, a single-serve rice cooker, blinking lamps made with statues of Confucius and the Immortals. While others took breaks at the steelyard, Dad soldered his paper name, You Thin Toy, a long weight of a sentence that I have on my writing desk now.

I've seen his photos at sea: He's a carefree sailor proudly posing with a GI. Below deck, he's a shirtless laundryman with a hot belligerence in his eye.

In one, he leans jauntily against a flagpole; in another he wields a wet mop like a heavy *guandao* over one shoulder. Dad's shown Wendy his tears, and he's allowed me to know his rage. He's taught us to make a weapon out of anything. His English, learned by being cursed at, has taught me everything about language.

Going to sea gave him something he couldn't find on land. He'd stay up all night making radios and other inventions. Mom would be furious that there was no room to serve breakfast. We inherited his creative temperament and, as well, Mom's tenacious work ethic.

All of Dad's best friends were sailors, flamboyant and eccentric adventurers, everyone an untamed post-Exclusion husband. Whenever Mr. Louie visited, his first question was, "When were you in Finland?" I loved how Mr. Gong's dragon tattoo crawled up his inner forearm, how it chased the immortal pearl that hid in the crook of his elbow, but I couldn't understand why he kept saying the number four, till finally—Four with Unkempt Hair—Liverpool! It made sense. Sailors were the cultural disseminators, broadcasting things like early rock and roll from port to port.

Antony remembered it being Dad's last voyage that he came home from the South Pacific with a shield-sized green sea turtle shell that barely fit under his arm. The brothers kept making eyes at each other till Antony finally asked, "Isn't that illegal?"

As Dad neared sixty, the work on the ships became harder and he took whatever jobs he could get on land. Once, I drove him to work at a Chinese restaurant in a town named Haystack, where "room and board" meant sleeping on the floor of an unfurnished house. I won't forget how one worker looked at me. I can still feel his disdain. He saw a college student and the look on his face said: What kind of daughter lets her father work like this?

One year, not long after my sister flew to Hawaii for a summer at the University of Hawaii, Dad signed on to work on the SS *Independence*, which cruised the Hawaiian Islands. Wendy visited him and after Dad showed her his bunk, he took her into the kitchen, asking the captain before scooping her some ice cream. She ate it, all the while thinking, *I'm not a kid.* After she said goodbye to Dad, the captain followed her and asked her out. I don't want to imagine the militaristic testosterone environment Dad endured.

The brothers had time with Dad. He showed them how to cast a crab net, how to make a paper kite soar, how to build a radio and work a wood saw, and how to fix their bikes. Every Saturday he took Tim to watch gung fu movies, and these would later become Tim's comfort. When Antony got his Camaro, he took Dad for a cruise on the Golden Gate

Bridge before the cement barriers were put up—to show him how fast it could go. After, Dad said, "You don't have to do that again."

He taught the brothers which weapon to carry, a retractable baton or the thinnest folding blade, also whether to conceal it on their body, behind the waistband, or under the driver's seat.

Mom herself said that without English they were relegated to salary work: seamanship and sweatshop labor, and with nowhere to lay down their humiliation, discontent fell onto their marriage. Soon Dad turned on Tim. Was I the only one who remembered that Dad had been dead-set against it when Mom wanted to send her last baby to be raised in Hong Kong by Grandmah? Dad's harshness toward his youngest was incomprehensible to me.

So little brother looked up to big brother, admiring Anthony's drawing talent, his stamina on their marathon bike races through Mount Tamalpais and the Marin Headlands. Antony gave Tim the name Bubblehead, but he always took care of his brother.

There was the time Tim left his car keys in a pizzeria and his Honda was stolen. Antony drove him through the Richmond and Sunset Districts until they found his stolen car in front of a driveway near Ocean Beach. Before dawn, the brothers were parked down the block to wait. When the hooligan came out of his house, the brothers tackled him. Antony held the thief down and told Tim to call the cops.

Tim was helium voiced when the thug reached behind the driver's seat for a tire iron.

More than nerve, it was the muscle of self-reliance that was passed on by Dad.

In adolescence, the brothers fought with a rancor that rivaled our parents' battles. There was the night one brother pummeled the other; I don't remember which did the pummeling and which received it. It wasn't their viciousness that shocked me but rather Dad's intervention. I watched as Dad stood there. I saw him wait and then, like a martial artist, step into their locked grip and dip an elbow deep into one son's throat. To emphasize the power unleashed here: this seaman move is a variation of the carotid hold we would all later see used on George Floyd.

* *

As a child, I didn't know enough English, but more importantly I didn't have enough life experience to understand business contracts, so I made mistakes, bad, yet innocent. On the freeway, I didn't know that Army Street wasn't spelled as it sounded—"are-me"—and we missed our exit. In junior high, I didn't understand insurance premiums and policies, and we got cheated. In high school, I compromised my parents' laundry business negotiations because, wanting to go out with friends, I rushed through translating the contract. There is no forgiving that I made trouble for my parents' already difficult lives.

Why is Deh crying? Why is Mah fuming?

I learned that there was no time to be afraid and no tolerance for tentativeness. When my sister said she looked up to me, I knew she wasn't looking down on our parents but rather doing them the courtesy of not bothering them. Bothering me was fine.

When we moved out of Chinatown, we were one of two Chinese homeowners on our block. A few doors from us lived a white family with boys who were about the same age as the brothers. Antony was nine, so Tim must have been six; they'd gotten bikes and were having fun exploring the neighborhood. When those boys yelled obscenities at the brothers, the parents continued drinking their Coors on their stoop, even laughing. Again—there was no bothering our parents. I went up to the red-faced man and his pink-thighed wife and repeated all the unkind words their children used.

"Do you think that's right?" I demanded.

A few days later, Dad was on a ladder fixing the roof of our two-story house. Wendy and I were gripping the lower rung of the stretched-out ladder when that freckled kid rode by spewing his garbage. The ladder rattled as Dad backed down it like a giant metal zipper and then chased that hooligan down the block.

We would not be bullied; that was the lesson.

Having witnessed the drama of Dad's Confession, the sisters changed their name back to his blood name, Ng. But the brothers kept his paper name, Toy. This wasn't about loyalty but rather practicality and paperwork. It was also about who would have to do the job (me). By the time the brothers were old enough to make the choice, it seemed that the worst of Exclusion and Confession had passed and like the amnesia that appears in ascending generations, it didn't seem worth the trouble.

When my first novel was published, Tim was working in the financial district and during his lunch hour was stopped by the *San Francisco Chronicle*'s Question Man, whose inquiry was on role models. Ever quick, Tim jumped in to give his opinion. That evening, I got calls from writer friends in California telling me that there was a Timothy Toy reading my book.

I laughed out loud before I told them, "That's my baby brother."

Regardless of legality, each of us took care of the parent we felt best capable of providing for. Ability mandated allegiance. Loyalty was also controlled by their discord in marriage. When our parents' fiftieth anniversary came up in 1998, we were shocked that Mom wanted a banquet.

"What for?" I said, which infuriated her.

She told me, "You expect happiness to lead to celebration, but I want endurance to be the emblem that marked our half-century union."

What a worthless daughter I was, refusing to give my mother the prize she wanted for surviving the marriage.

* *

As I sit with my father's body, his color is waning and I can feel the skin on his hands pulling back onto his bones, so I consider: How to forgive?

After Tim died, Antony's friends finally relinquished his number and it feels like dynamite in my phone. I want to honor my father so I call the number. When it goes to voice message, I tell my brother to come and pay his last respects.

I touch Dad's clasped hands and use Antony's Chinese name to tell him, "Your son is coming."

Our father had a monk's palate (maybe it was all that seafaring food). He preferred salt and sun-cured over man-frozen and forbade us to eat anything with preservatives or food coloring. At restaurants, he hollered at waiters about MSG, calling it rat poison. In respect of this, my sister and I reject embalming. On his sixtieth birthday, our mother had insisted that we children present our father with his burial suit. I know where this suit is in his closet, but I can't bear to have strangers disturb his body. On my knees, I ask for pardon.

Will Antony come?

The first time Dad went into hospice, we had no number for Antony so Wendy sent him a certified letter, which was returned. A neighbor had seen Dad being brought home in an ambulance after his stroke and must have told

Antony. My brother spent that single visit on the phone with his wife.

My sister lost hope first because she's not one to waste love. What's wrong with me?

I'd appreciated Antony's wife. She'd cared enough that she called me in New York to ask how to assuage the bitterness between my parents; she felt it was impeding Mom's struggle against her cancer. In my decades away, in my three-thousand-miles escape I'd finally had to accept there was no hope. I can't expect an outsider to fully comprehend the brutal destruction of their marriage, how many years had my hope risen and fallen like fists? Marrying into a family cannot give one full entry into its complex love and pain. But that she'd tried was goodwill that I didn't take for granted.

All I knew was Mom's intention: four kids, four flats. Mom managed to save and buy another house, at full market price. It was a mirror-copy of the family home. Her intention was to set her first son up for his own family and it's where Antony and his family live now.

Tim told me that he'd walked in several times while Antony was in hushed conversation with Mom and eventually figured out that he wanted Mom to remove her name from the deed, to sign it over to him and his wife. I was in New York those years, so I never heard anything about it. Did she sign so as not to be cut off from her grandchildren? It was Antony's absolute refusal to be in communication with us that felt like a betrayal. Probably he had reasons and maybe the secrets were a form of protection. Now that Mom and Dad and Tim are gone, what does it matter?

What's horrible to live with is that I failed to protect my mother. Then I felt my mother's admonishment: You are the eldest. Lead in forgiveness.

So I will hold this dear: whatever agony Antony suffers for choosing his wife and children over a family long broken, I must not judge. If I offer trust, if I soften into love, I will not damage hope.

I have no choice but to wait on Antony to act. Waiting is never precise. I can't know the pain he swallows or the pain he inflicts. I cannot imagine his anguish or understand what loyalties force his choices, but I can respect it.

I will wait.

* *

The phone rings: Antony. We have no preliminaries, no pleasantries, just familyspeak, getting-things-done instructions. This isn't coldness; this is immigrant efficiency.

I make my way downstairs and sit on the cracked marble of the last step, the only damage from the Loma Prieta earthquake, which struck on Mom's lunar birthday, her year without longevity noodles.

My phone rings: the mortuary apologizing for bridge traffic.

Antony arrives and, as always, is quick to smile. I notice his graying temples, hear an odd click in his jaw when he greets me. He is still lanky, carrying his 6'4" frame well. We embrace. Then I just tell him what he has to do.

My brother gives me a perplexed look. "I never heard that before."

"Yep," I insist. "Mom told me."

It was my inspired lie. I owed it to Dad to make it right, and maybe I owed Antony something that absolved his absence.

I offer to perform the ritual again. I don't mention that hearing is the last sense to leave the dead. As a boy, he was meticulous about decisions, weighing everything, so I gave him time. He couldn't have had it easy coming after his tough, *buu-bui* bossy sisters.

"I'll do it." Antony nods.

I'm not surprised, but I'm ready to insist and, of course, to fight. I stand back as my brother prepares himself, observing the sandy layer of dust on his boots, the dip of the toe plate. I watch how methodically he undoes his laces and feel a sudden tenderness. Antony drops to his knees, crawling over the threshold. His cries of *Deh! Deh!* fill the house. Then silence. Time stops and I hear the four-year-old brother I've always adored. "Hi, Dad."

My rancor dissolves. Forgiveness isn't what I need; what I want is a road on which to continue. I lost a brother. A lost brother returned.

The men from the mortuary arrive with solemn brows, slick hair, and gloved hands; they move like thieves. They prepare us for what is to happen: the sheet, the black bag, and the gurney. One says, "Some find this part upsetting, you might want to look away."

I'm not looking away. As his daughter, I will protect my father. As a writer, I want to see it all.

Antony steps up to the body. "Dad, I'm going home now. I'm going to cook the rice."

I ask why this send-off, and he shrugs. "That's what Dad used to say when he got tired of me. 'Go home, go make dinner.'"

We follow the gurney out the door, down the stairs, and into the cold street. The wind bites, a thick fog rolls in, and we stand in it watching until the van carrying our father vanishes.

21

Mom's cancer was diagnosed just after 9/11; it was a scary time to fly but when there was a chance to get her into an experimental study, I flew out from New York and kept flying back for each treatment. I flew so much I had a getaway bag and a uniform. I wore the same dark dress with pockets until too many businessmen asked for water. I got tired of saying "I don't work here."

Friends asked why I didn't let the brothers take care of Mom. The idea had never crossed my mind because as the eldest, that was my job. Now I know that my insistence on doing everything dismissed my siblings. Ner pointed out, "You doing everything doesn't make them feel better." My sister had also been saying since childhood, "Mom and Dad are always waiting for you."

Why wouldn't my brothers be angry? All their lives, they had to ask Big Sister for her opinion, for permission. As much as I resented being responsible, they must have resented being powerless, or useless in the eyes of Mom and Dad who always said, Let's wait till Fae comes home.

When Mom died, I relinquished my role. I told the brothers to make the funeral plans. I knew we would fight and things would be awful if we tried to work together. To keep what little was left in our relationship, I asked them to take care of it. But to them, it was like I didn't care.

It only got more awful. The brothers were bamboozled into a feudal Confucian ceremony. Wendy was horrified: I felt guilty I didn't fix it. There was an altar with a huge pig's head, a whole chicken, bowls of rice, giant punks of incense, nine blankets, and nonstop bowing, which called for daughters coming after the brothers.

After the burial, we had to go back to the house for another ceremony before going to the comfort dinner. Antony's wife still had not said a word to me the whole day and now still refused to look at me, and the third time she passed me without an address, I said, "You bitch."

If that's the reason why Antony cut us off, maybe I can't blame him.

I'd had it and wanted to head back to the desert, but Ner suggested we spend the day with Dad, take him for dim sum, maybe a drive across the Golden Gate. Ner had checked the weather and there was a warning about tule fog.

I said no, we headed out, and sure enough, tule fog descended and closed the Grapevine. We exited at Lebec and saw a nursery and stepped inside. The dwarf nectarine trees greeted us. I smiled, the blooming vermillion flowers would have pleased Mom, so I got the pair and Ner managed to fit them into the packed Jag.

Even in the desert, Ner could grow anything. My first meal there, I'd looked at the grilled scallions and parsnips and said, "These aren't vegetables." The next time I arrived, he'd grown vines of snow peas, long string beans, three kinds of mustard greens, and a crop of fuzzy melons. All summer, we'd eat mirin corn—like candy—right from the stalk. At dusk, we walked through the peach grove to pick white, cling, freestone, nectarine, and donut, and that ripe first bite with the desert wind was sublime. Kabocha grew late into the fall and lasted us through the winter. One December, Ner surprised me with a winter melon, frosty green and lantern shaped—my Christmas melon.

Instead of cypress, ocotillo lined the long driveway. The thorny whip-like sticks cut up toward the desert sky until late May when the blood-orange flowers bloomed from their tips. Then they became colossal candlesticks with fiery blossoms flickering in the hot dryness. It was our own tree sanctuary.

There were ten-foot spreads of prickly pears that hummingbirds nested in. In the back, groupings of crested cacti, collections of rare San Pedros, and a hothouse of exotic succulents. My favorite was the trio of palo verde trees with fronds that shimmered like a river when the Santa Ana winds roared through. In the back, facing toward the San Gabriel Mountains, was a row of smoke trees, considered invasive and named the Forbidden Trees. At the ends of their thin branches were puffs, like bursts of smoke from a gun. During one of the many fire evacuations that were already starting in early 2000s, I saw how they'd grown into a thick purple-and-red hedge, waving as wild as the distant walls of fire.

The fires scared me. Then, Dad was getting lost outside so I decided to move to Berkeley—to keep an eye on him. Ner took the dwarf nectarines trees, along with the dozen golden barrels and hundreds of rare cacti to his land in the Santa Cruz Mountains.

Soon, Ner noticed that the nectarine trees were suffering and suggested they might do better in San Francisco. I thought about it. At the time, Tim was maintaining Mom's garden and had taken on her passion for growing things. Perhaps because Tim had Mom the least, it forced him to be more patient, to wait his turn, to be the one to forgive. Even though he and Dad didn't communicate, Tim's presence upstairs was a form of protection; Tim kept watch. Perhaps as the last one, my brother had the braver, deeper love.

Mom's memorial trees with Tim?

Why not?

In late March, when the trees could best tolerate a transition, Ner and I rented a U-Haul and moved the two-hundred-pound planters from his land to the front of my old family house. The trees were as tall as me, with an expanse of branches that I couldn't wrap my arms around. Ner threw burlap over the craggy branches, and I tied them down with twine. When I stepped back to admire their bouffant heads, I felt something fly away.

I climbed in the van and spread out the blankets. Ner made a ramp, lifted the planters onto a dolly, and wheeled them into the van. He lowered the trees as if they were gigantic eggs. Then he bound rope around their trunks, making intricate knots that reminded me of my father's ingenuity at creating tools when none existed, and secured the rope to the anchor bars of the van. Ensuring there would be no trauma to the trees, he drove the coastal route. Light was starting to skim across the ocean as we got onto the Pacific Coast Highway. The U Haul hugged the shoreline and the skies peaked wide as the calm green ocean poured out to the line of no return. I rolled down my windows to take in the sting of the sea.

We were lone travelers, not a single camper, SUV, Volvo wagon, or tour bus was in sight for mile after winding mile. Every cypress was salt tortured, every pine arm rigid to the wind. Passing through the magnificent and treacherous Devil's Slide, I wondered not why I left, but why I stayed away so long.

When I introduced my sister to Ner, her welcome was exquisite. "We've all wanted her back home in California, but you're the only one that could do it."

Once we got onto the sandy stretch of the Great Highway, I called Tim and told him we had a surprise and to meet us outside in five minutes.

Turning onto Twenty-Ninth Avenue, my six-foot tall brother was standing in front of the house, neck craned, wearing the shearling slippers I'd sent for his birthday. I got out and yelled at him.

"What?" He shrugged. "They're warm."

"They're practically new!" I swatted him again.

When Ner swung open the back doors, Tim was speechless. The men wrestled the huge planters off the van and wheeled them to the front of the house.

I watched how intently Tim turned the planters left and right, then more left, looking for the perfect angle so that the branches made a bowl to catch the sunlight.

"That good?" I asked.

"Let's try it there." Tim nodded. "Let's see how they do."

Ner had suggested that this trip be all about Tim, but I was skeptical. There was no visit without seeing Dad too. But once I saw Tim so happy, I felt happy too—and got into the van. As Ner started driving off, I looked back until I could no longer see my brother by the trees.

The next morning, Tim called to tell me he'd slept in the front room, that every time he heard a truck, he went to the window to check that the trees were still there. I detailed what the thieves would have to do: rent a truck, get a dolly, wait until the dead of the night, haul them away without disturbing any witnesses.

"A lot of trouble," I said.

Tim's flat is lighter and airier than Dad's downstairs. A long rectangular window stretches across the front room with a single sheet of glass. There's a line of eucalyptus trees that shade Presidio Middle School two blocks away, and due south, a lone Chinese pine stands proud in the mist of our Outside Lands section of San Francisco.

The dwarf nectarine trees that now stand guard in front of our family home journeyed a long way for the job. I never had a chance to tell Tim that they were a tribute to our mother, but my brother received the trees with such gratitude, I know he felt her love.

This is continuation, our family in trees.

* *

It took over a decade for the grip of sorrow to loosen from our family brocade.

One day, at dim sum, my father asked, "What did your mother say before she went on the road?" I told him what I thought would make him happy.

"Mom said to take care of you."

Dad smiled and I knew what he was thinking because I'd spent a lifetime reading his mind: You, my daughter, are a liar. Talk Big Words. No surprise that novels are called Little Words, Small Talk.

It unsettled me and I didn't visit for another week. When I did, I took Dad to dim sum so we could eat and not talk.

As I poured the tea, Dad told me, "Your mother visited me in a dream." His smile was genuine, and he seemed pleased with the visitation. "Your mother misses me."

I couldn't help what came out of my mouth. "Liar!"

"It's true! She told me, since you're sleeping so much, why not come to the netherworld and keep me company?"

My father winked and then I broke into a laugh like Laffing Sal and Dad joined me.

22

TIM'S GARDEN has become an oasis. As the Yoshino trees blossom, their petals float like popcorn in Yang Guifei's bath. The dwarf nectarine trees flower and the bird of paradise with its orange head is a bird on call. A purple rosebush in the center gives up a dozen blooms every season, a delicious treat for Mister Dewdrop.

Years before, Tim and I were here together. He was showing me his new plantings, and I remember my brother was calm and I was patient enough to stand still, to listen.

It was mid-February, and the trees were just beginning to bud. The sun was out and I heard a low pitch ringing, like distant bells. Tim told me it was the wind. "The cables of the Golden Gate Bridge touching. You've been gone a long time."

Then my brother pointed out where he wanted to plant his new cherry trees, the rhododendrons, the rosebush, the grasses for his tortoises, and the sunniest patch for the spring sunflowers—all his plans for the rest of the garden, Mom's garden. Suddenly his eyes followed a bird into a distant pine.

"That's probably the descendent of the original blue jay Dad saved." Tim told me the story about the hurt bird with a droopy wing. A splint made of toothpicks. Tim giggled describing how Dad fed the hurt bird Po Chai Pills.

We laughed about those brown pills, pellets our parents gave us for tummy aches, nausea, headaches, seasickness, and diarrhea. If we complained, we had to take the stinky pills, so we made sure never to get sick, or we never complained.

Tim laughed. "Just opening the vial made me want to throw up."

"How'd he get the bird to swallow it?" I asked.

"I held it and Dad squeezed open its mouth," he said.

"I never knew that story."

Tim shrugged.

Then we were quiet.

✻ ✻

When my father no longer had an appetite, I made him a bowl of winter: pine nuts boiled for hours with anise stars. The licorice scent wafted through the house and woke him.

"Is that pine?" he called out from the sunroom.

I took the bowl to the warmest room of the house. "You used to make us this winter treat. Remember how we fought to find the biggest pine nut?"

My father nodded. "A pine has no fear."

"Trees have fear?" I was perplexed.

As he scooped his hand through the bowl, the pine nuts sounded like falling rain. "The pine isn't afraid of winter. No matter how cold, it grows straight, no matter how windy, its branches never break."

He told me that as a young boy, he'd watched squirrels pluck the nuts from the cones, hide them inside their cheeks, then climb up the pine to tuck away for the winter. "Then I knew their secret place," he said.

"You stole their harvest?" I asked.

He winked. "But I paid them back with water."

I found the plumpest nut, cracked it, and peeled off its thin membrane and placed the fleshy teardrop into his palm. My father studied it from every angle and then told me about how snow and pine were best friends.

"Snow breaks the branches of a cypress but slips through the pine's long branches. Snow collects at its trunk and melts in the spring to nourish both trees."

His voice became both light and weighty: "When you bury your father, plant a pine tree nearby. The pine will offer companionship and keep the demon Wang Xiang from eating my *noh*."

I took my father's hand.

I hold his knowledge.

* *

It's not only my father's mind that I want to preserve. When he relinquished his desire to be buried in China, he acquiesced to become the American father for eternity.

In our apartment at the Villa Rosa, Great-Grandfather's tablet was his name written on a strip of rice paper. In my writing office, I've made our ancestral tablet with the oldest photograph of the family in China. The backdrop is a mansion that looks French. The four young men who stand in the back row seem to be cadets; they wear military field jackets. Three elderly women in dark clothing sit in the center of the middle row. On each side, a pair of younger women in light-colored dresses sit with children on their laps. On the far left is the only woman without a child, this is Grandmah's sister. My grandmother sits next to her and in her arms, my mother is an infant wearing a cap and holding a jangle. This tells me it is 1929. The children are on the floor, three girls in long dresses and knee socks, two boys in Boy Scouts' uniforms with epaulettes.

There are no old men. There are no young husbands.

May this tablet protect our knowledge from being devoured by demons.

III.

DEPARTING

Father, Mother, and Great-Grandfather

23

ANCESTRAL TABLET

A Husband's Words to His Wife

In my bachelor year, I came to the school and observed you from afar. Later, you would tell me that you saw me at the edge of the courtyard, not my person but the light from the stone on my ring. That refracted light caught your heart. Your face glowed as you told me how you'd never imagined a jewel throwing brightness so far. That day, when your eyes followed that diamond light toward me, I saw a girl so young she still played paper shuttle games.

I wasn't like the other bachelors who enjoyed the gambling dens and teahouses; I preferred being alone and bought a pair of

songbirds to take for walks along the riverbank. After I met all the prospective brides,
I chose you, an orphan. I didn't, as others did, pursue marriage to increase family
wealth. Instead, I chose a bride to decrease
all that family sorrow hanging between us
both.

24

ANCESTRAL TABLET

A Mother's Words to Her Eldest

When my time comes, your sister will cry, and I will not be able to walk the road. Lead her aside so I can go.

As my firstborn, I gave you my trust. You took care of the others, and this made your character. Then, like me, you left your mother and made your own life. As I bore my mother's hardships, you witnessed mine. Life. A mother gives. A mother is owed.

Your father's story captured me, and I bequeathed it to you. I did not tell the others. You would grow into the business of stories but you already understood: stories are dangerous. Always keep something for yourself; this preserves desire, the seed of all loving.

Whatever he endured in America was nothing compared to what he'd survived in China. I calculated my affinity; what is the worth of family? Without me he'd be the Orphan Bachelor begging restaurant scraps, wandering Dupont, squandering his days in gambling parlors.

I bore him four treasures, but my true labor was bearing his running away. All those years he took to sea to escape his family, I endured it because he was the boy who could not cry his way home; every home became a prison.

My daughter, I bequeath no gold, only this hard eye: Do not love in pity. Throw grief into the ocean and let the Queen Mother of the Four Seas take the man who asks and asks.

You waited till just a few hours before your impending marriage to call so I only had time to tell you about the magical creature I saw before my own wedding. At the riverbank, the sky was overcast, the air humid, rain was coming. Behind the thick clouds, something flickered and I saw a long-winged creature, its tail a brush writing hope into the sky. I kept the vision a secret until I crossed the ocean of peace.

I cried tears of worry and want. "One hundred years of happiness, one hundred ascending visions." You were displeased.

I do not ask for explanation, and you do not need my forgiveness. This is the voyage of mothering. I want your heart safe in another's embrace before I ascend my road.

25

I AM the eldest daughter of the eldest daughter of another eldest daughter.

Without children of my own, the lineage of the *baa bai* eldest daughter—the take-charge girl—ends with me.

The last time I saw my mother, I brought her a thin-skinned orange. As I placed it in her palm, I asked if she remembered the Lunar New Year when I returned home with nothing in hand.

"Mah remembers."

Mother also forgave.

When the caregiver urged her to speak my name, my mother's voice was opium-rich as she said the name that she herself gave me: the ideogram for intelligence, the word meaning "brightness." Light. Light. Beaming hope.

I whispered into my mother's ear. I uttered her word of adoration: *haahn*, the word she'd always used to express love. "Mah, I embrace you for life. Mah, I *haahn* you with all my life."

Hospice advised me to use the word "goodbye." To give permission. "You can go."

I could not translate that sentiment, so I did not use their words. This child will not tell her mother what to do, when to go.

When I took my mother's hand, a phrase from childhood returned, a hopeful, affectionate, even romantic expression of farewell, like *arrivederci. Hau wui jau kei.* May we have the fortune to meet again. 後會有期.

I closed one hand over the other, extending my clasped fist like a disciple saying farewell to the master. My mother was ascending the mountain.

"Mah," I caressed her. "Mah, I love you so much, I will see you again."

Dear Great and Honorable Mother, below whose knee I prostrate:

In the time since you've walked your road, I've lived with two of your sentences. They are dear to me for the mystery of you. These sentences are about my father. No, they're about your husband.

In the first, you speak directly about your pleasure: "Skin so soft on his arm, and more alongside his thigh."

The second sentence is about your union and about mothering. "Together we've raised four children, yet he still doesn't love me."

Mother, you speak about love, but instead of your usual *haahn*—the veiled word, meaning "embrace"—you use the word *oi*, meaning "love." It's an unusual construction for a Chinese sentence but I know that you are fitting the Western intimacy you've learned in this country into what you've always desired, abiding love.

With this translation, you married stoic immigrant loyalty with free pioneer love and made an American sentence.

As your firstborn, you let me see more. When I was too young to comprehend your feelings, you told me to hold memory aside, to trust time. Like gold, feelings get brighter. That lesson has not only taught me about writing but it has also kept you dearly by my side.

Mother, today I am the elder in your stead and I remember your last words, which I had hid for fear of feeling your loneliness. What you told me now shines: "A mother owes because she brings forth life. Debt is not a burden but a joy."

Your First Girl

EPILOGUE

With youngest brother

J UST BEFORE I started at Washington High, we moved out of Chinatown. Everything came with us: stove and icebox, decades of the *Chinese Times*, scrap metal from Dad's job at Bethlehem Steel, and every bit of saved cloth from Mom's sweatshop. Over the years, we collected more stuff, desks and tables, three industrial machines from Mom's sweatshop, bookshelves and lamps, old dishes and woks, a popcorn popper, cake mixer, and the life-size stuffed bear Dad won at the Sacramento fair. Coming from a land of famine and strife—and no fun, my sister adds—my parents saved everything as an expression of hope. One day these objects will fulfill their noble function. Everything was packed up and taken to our new home in the Outer Richmond.

✳ ✳

After three decades in New York, I've moved back to the family house, which is now over a hundred years old. Mom first, then Tim, then Dad passed here. I was living and teaching at Berkeley, but my sister insisted I move into what she now calls the Tomb.

The house is located in the Outside Lands, which was all sand dunes until 1870 when land was annexed to build Golden Gate Park and the dunes were subdued. Our parents bought the house at an estate auction in 1972 when it was less than prime real estate. The house is two blocks away from the tony Seacliff enclave.

A seamstress and a sailor, how did they afford the 10 percent cash deposit and manage to hold on to a property that even unmaintained as we speak is still worth well over a million plus?

For several years already, I've been trying to empty the house—the lower flat where Dad was living and Tim's upper flat, where I now live. After Mom died, Tim cleared the downstairs family flat and tucked everything not immediately useful into the many crevices of the garage, and for a year, I just filled the bins every Tuesday night.

My only rule was to keep everything with Dad's handwriting. There's a lot of it: Dad wrote on everything, in journals, on edges of newspapers, menus from the American President Lines, receipts and napkins. It will take focused attention to go through it all.

Everything else—I've separated into the worthy and the worthless.

Are these worthy?

The burial jade from Taipei City's night market. The bamboo cricket cage from Kowloon City. Simon and Garfunkel's *Bridge over Troubled Water*. I'm keeping the stacks of newspapers and clipped articles in a pile because I've already found bills slipped between stories of Mao and of atrocities in America.

Time to dump the worthless.

A railroad track? The Israeli gas mask with instructions in Hebrew that I offered to my friend Mali who remembered using the same in the eighties when Saddam Hussein was bombing Tel Aviv—she declined. The spools of colored threads like a kaleidoscope of Life Savers, thick and thin coils of ribbons like a box of donuts? Tins and tins of buttons that Mom never threw out because superstition warned that discarded buttons brought forth bellyaches. Was it because buttons looked like belly buttons? No time and no one to ask now.

What about Dad's long Flavin-like fluorescent tubes? The woodland of doors, the boxes of doorknobs, the used and sparkly sheets of sandpaper, the cartons of incandescent bulbs? The antique two-man manual tree saw from Germany? Boxes of copper fittings, jars of old screws, coils of hoses? Our teenage bikes with flat tires, Dad's half-fixed radios, cassette players with a collection of Cantonese opera recordings, no time to look for a Mulan reel. What about his butterfly harp, his two-string erhu, the violin, a banjo! The flutes he made from bamboo and steel pipes?

And his creations from his seafaring days: miniature rice cookers, one-person fans, the lamp made from a large wooden Buddha, and clocks from around the world.

Time to be ruthless. I don't pick up the same object twice. What is it? Is it useful? If not, out it goes.

Giant Christmas balls, cute ornaments then but space hogs now. Out they go. A vase. Is that a chip on the rim? Out. Platform shoes, miniskirts, Halloween costumes. All out.

The spindly spider plant, a dried-out Hawaiian ti-plant log, the climbing ivy vines choking out the good feng shui, they all don't deserve to live. Out. Out. Out.

But what got me was the least-traveled item—a dusty bottle of Johnnie Walker Black left from our long-ago family banquets at the once-elegant, now-shuttered Tao Tao. The dark bottle, still in its cellophane sleeve, makes me wonder if our happy times might be wrapped up and saved somewhere too.

Once the bins are full, the fun part is to climb in and stomp it down so I can fill it back up. But I need to turn off my sister's voice. Last month, I made the mistake of bragging to her that I was paying the price of one haul with two cans worth of junk; she didn't laugh and the next week, I got a *lai see*, ten crisp one-hundred-dollar bills wrapped in a red envelope with her curt note: "Get new shoes."

After dragging the heavy bins to the curb, I'm the queen of accomplishment. I take Johnnie upstairs with me, I shower, and, waiting for my dinner to arrive, I crack the bottle open and let the whiskey warm me, expanding and then shrinking memories as I start shredding Social Security records, pay stubs, and utility bills.

What I'm still looking for is Great-Grandfather's bankbook with his American name.

* *

Living in the family home, I've discovered a new generation of Orphan Bachelors, Danny and Derrick, the bachelor brothers next door, an old man who walks his lame dog in all weather, and the Wheelchair Bachelor who lives up the hill. Tim had told me about how he guns his wheelchair like a hot rod, often stopping to admire the trees or using them as his ashtray.

Figuring out my own rhythm in the neighborhood—shopping, post office, library, gym—I've figured out the Wheelchair Bachelor's too. When I see him using a large Rilakkuma Japanese bear as a backrest, I know it's a Bingo win from On Lok Senior Center. After the gym, I sometimes stop at Lung Fung Bakery for a custard tart, but it's really to see if I can catch the Wheelchair Bachelor for a chance chat. Often, he's in the middle of a loud chess game, but he's not the kind of man you can approach without a good reason. His isn't a laborer's face and there's nothing simple about his gaze. The broad plane of his warlord forehead says he's got a plan in mind and there's an exit map in his eye. He drags on his cigarette in that feudal way, letting it hang low, sucking hard, eyes downcast with intent, he's taking in more than tobacco.

Leaving the house late one afternoon, I see the Wheelchair Bachelor in front of the nectarine trees. I greet him with the familiar and familial, "Ah Goong."

He doesn't respond, so I repeat, "Grandfather, good day?"

He nods. "*Ho.*"

Then he looks directly into my eyes. He doesn't speak, but the words have been invited and are louder than if spoken: *I knew your brother.*

When he motors off, I watch him, the ear tops of the furry bear bouncing just below his shoulder blades.

A neighbor told me that the Wheelchair Bachelor has an institutionalized son. That's a story I do not want to know.

* *

This father-son story Dad told my sister and me is unforgettable. I was almost ten and had heard enough of his stories to have an expectation, but this one was told like an opera: melodramatic, loud, and practically impossible to follow.

Father Sima Tan was the court historian under the rule of Emperor Wudi of the Western Han dynasty. He recorded the astronomical conditions to the emperor, who used the secret movements of the solar and lunar eclipses, the rising and falling of tidal waves, earthquake frequencies, and wind events to determine the course of his governing.

Reporting on the sky theater bored Father Sima Tan. What he really wanted to do was write China's two-thousand-year history, so he started his opus, taking notes and making an outline.

"But then he died!" Dad shouted, and I was shocked too.

"At the deathbed, Son Sima Qian is bequeathed his father's deadline. Talk about an inheritance. Talk about filial piety!" Dad laughed.

So much drama, we needed an intermission.

Dad continued about the emperor conquering more kingdoms and acquiring more gifts. The Ferghana horses from Central Asia were Dad's favorite and he drew them with their big round barrels, powerful crests, and short, straight forelegs. Dad's drawings of those "heavenly horses" were in our bedroom, the kitchen, living room, and the smallest horse alone in the short hallway.

"Horses everywhere," Mom complained. "It's a stampede!"

And like all trophies, the horses were fussy eaters, and endless meadows of heirloom alfalfa had to be cultivated to keep them happy.

Meanwhile, there were constant invasions from the north, so the emperor sent a general to lure and kill the invaders. The general lured them, but the barbarians surrounded him, and when the promised reinforcement troops never arrived, his five thousand troops were slaughtered.

"Surrendering was treason," Dad explained. "He should have committed suicide."

The emperor slaughtered the general's entire family.

"Did the general die too?" my sister asked.

"Everyone dies," I said.

When I heard that Sima Qian spoke up for the disgraced general, I knew it was hopeless. Sima Qian's choice was castration or death. Castration! Otherwise, how would he finish his father's book?

It doesn't end yet because his friend Ren An also offended the emperor and wrote to Sima Qian for help.

"What's wrong with this emperor?" my sister piped in.

Letter to Ren An is Sima Qian's reply to his friend. In it, Sima expresses his regret for his friend's dilemma, explaining that he could not insult the emperor again, as he needed to complete his manuscript.

"A man has only one death. That death may be as weighty as Mount Tai or it may be as light as a goose feather. It all depends on the way he uses it."

Today, *Letter to Ren An* is studied as a classic in Chinese literature. As a child, the history and the vow of loyalty moved me. Now, I'm also moved by how it weaves together friendship and writing. When my father first told me about it, I was too young to fully comprehend the consequences of history on a life, but I felt my father's awe, so I *copied* his admiration. Many years later, I found the translation and even though I read it in the barbarian's language, I was transported back to that afternoon when my father first told it to me. My awe was now complete.

Sima Qian's devotion to progeny makes him the original Orphan Bachelor, and his dedication to history makes him my literary forefather.

As well, the entire Sima clan is filled with heroes. Ancestor Sima Tan who dreamed up the book of history, Son Sima Qian who finished his father's book, the granddaughter who protected her father's manuscript from the emperor, and the great-grandson who presented the book to the world, and perhaps might be the true author of *Letter to Ren An*.

✽ ✽

After completing my own manuscript, I considered: Who would read this? I won't be hurt if my sister doesn't. She's read my other books and has said, "I know where you got everything." This is intimacy. Antony's an electrician and before he read my first book, he prepared himself, and told me, "I want to concentrate." This moved me, as if the currents of fact and fiction were dangerously crucial to him. Perhaps, if he doesn't read this book, we might be saved from the firepower of more misunderstanding. Tim would have read it first—and fast—laughing at all the secrets. Nelson, my brother-in-law, is a prosthodontist who makes works of art to work in the body—noses, ears, and eyes so detailed, the lashes flutter. Perhaps this is how a book should work in the body: useful, as well as artful.

* *

As my father neared his own death, he became more and more like the ancients, speaking in parables and idioms, storing truth in his belly, guarding and protecting us from his depository of discontent. The lore, the mythmaking, and maybe even the flat-out making-it-all-up are now our story.

In his final years, I stopped trying to read his mind or guess his needs; I accepted that his true desires would always evade me. Perhaps this was the best road. I can see him winking, hear his gentle chiding: Not all has to be spoken or written, that the Superior one trusts the truth in the belly. Knowing did not involve feeling and feeling did not demand understanding. Attention was enough payment.

As I use the word "perhaps," I hear my father using the word "*pei you*." As a child, I understood it as his way of inviting possibility. Perhaps my father knew that Mom had told me his story and that by sidestepping that acknowledgement, he freed me. Perhaps leaving his story alone gave me the will to write it out of our lives.

Our Orphan Bachelors believed that perfection and completion were false markers on the road. When working in the gold mines, on the railroad, in the galleys of ships, the underbellies of kitchens, and the basements of sweatshops, what's important is to hold something back for the self; this is our blood of hope.

Perhaps Mah told me the story I needed to carry, and perhaps Deh didn't tell what would imprison me. Though written in the barbarian's language, may this manuscript translate to the song of everlasting hope that travels wordlessly back home.

AUTHOR'S NOTE

THIS BOOK of living memory is my recollection of experiences that occurred over the span of decades. Some names have been changed, some events have been compressed, and some dialogue has been re-created through translation.

Language is a living entity. Each generation transforms it, and each dialect becomes a language unto itself. Toishanese is one that's armed with *guandao* attitude.

In transliteration, inspiration is my guide. The reader may recognize a Canto-American vernacular and the current umbrella of Mandarin. With works that were important to my becoming a writer, I use the transliteration I learned (Li Po, Fa Mulan, Canton). When referring to modern events and figures, I use pinyin (Taiping Rebellion, Qing, Yang Guifei).

"*Hei*" is the Cantonese word meaning breath/mood/ energy. (Some readers may be familiar with it as "*chi*," or the more correct "*ch'i*" or "*qi*.") Throughout the book, "*hei*" is a nod, wink, and riff on the tenacious and loquacious spirit of the early Orphan Bachelors.

When I've taken creative liberties in recreating the colloquial Cantonese onto the page, I've aimed to provide clarity in context, with the hope and invitation that everyone will enjoy the wit, humor, and rebel-daring of our Orphan Bachelors. However, any mistakes and all confusions are mine.

ACKNOWLEDGMENTS

I AM GRATEFUL to Elisabeth Schmitz for her belief and support. Her brilliant editorial eye and piercing insights have lifted the manuscript to illuminate hope. Because of her, this has become a braver book, the book I dreamed of.

I thank Michele Mortimer for her dedication, tenacious advocacy, and the hep Ctown subtitle. Many thanks as well to Liz Darhansoff for welcoming me to her literary home.

Thank you, Paula Cooper Hughes for clarifying the language to reveal the story. Thank you, Lilly Sandberg, Julia Berner-Tobin, and every team member at Grove. Thank you, Morgan Entrekin.

Pamela Kyle Crossley took time from her own manuscript to consider mine; her early reading grounded the work and her last gave it the chance to soar. Gretel Ehrlich walked with my father and promised to bring him a herd next time. Patricia Mulcahy and I are the First Girls in our families; decades ago, she gave me the idea for this book. I'm grateful for her friendship and her writing camaraderie.

Thank you to the Rockefeller Foundation's Bellagio Center, the Guggenheim Foundation, and the Lannan Residency Fellowship. Thanks to Ellen Rosenbush and Marisa Siegal for publishing early sections of the manuscript.

Many books provided clarification, guidance, and inspired conversations. Among the numerous authors: Sarah Allan, Sucheng Chan, Gordon H. Chang, Mae Ngai, Shen Yung-Ken, Jing Tsu, Judy Yung, Yung Wing.

Thank you to my friends and family: Sara Antonelli, King-Kok Cheung, Patti Hiramoto, Maybelle Kagy, Barbara Klar, Shirley Louie, Nelson Lowe, Laiwan and Edmund Lowe, Katherine McNamara, my students, Jan Pang, Peggy Snow, Tony Toy, Anne Twitty, Khatharya Um, Akemi and Matt Wayne, Juvenda Wong, Sau-ling Wong, Shawn Hsu Wong, my JJ, Rosina Lee Yue. Again, and always, to Ner.